PRAISE FOR JO

The Boys of

"Reading Jo Ann Beard's prose feels as comfortable as falling into step beside an old, intimate friend. She's the sort of writer whose charm lies in the voice — a kitchen-table drawl entirely uncontaminated by sentimentality. . . . Beard remembers (or imagines) her childhood self with an uncanny lucidity that startles."

— LAURA MILLER, *New York Times Book Review*

"Utterly compelling . . . uncommonly beautiful. . . . The writing lifts the book into the stratosphere. . . . The key is a voice of equal parts curiosity and vulnerability. Life in these pages is an astonishment. . . . *The Boys of My Youth* speaks volumes about growing up female and struggling to remain true to yourself."

— DAN CRYER, *Newsday*

"Jo Ann Beard sustains an almost miraculous level of detachment as she describes the stuff of nightmares . . . and how she, and by implication all of us, survive them. . . . Beard evokes the dizzying sensation of tragedy, but she also provides weird, sparkling moments of grace and stillness. *The Boys of My Youth* evokes the mundane, the hilarious, the horrific, and the redemptive all taken together, the very rhythm of life."

— ELLEN KANNER, *Fort Lauderdale Sun-Sentinel*

"Beard remembers with beautiful simplicity the feeling of youthful longing, and combines those memories with the pains that accompany adult life."

— *Marie Claire*

"These stories do it all. They are smart, funny, and moving. They are personal and unique and also universal. . . . There is not a false note or wrong word."

— BARBARA FISHER, *Boston Globe*

"Truly extraordinary. . . . It's a daring act and also a bit of a magic trick to focus on a scrap of real life — a failed family vacation, a run-in with an irate driver, adolescent ridiculousness, a marriage on the skids — and manage to spin it into something sad and beautiful. Yet that is exactly what Beard does. . . . It is the simple fact that Beard gives voice to these small moments of sometimes sad, sometimes joyous truths — the all but forgotten time that composes the bulk of real life — that makes her writing so moving. . . . Beard finds, always and perfectly, the heartbreaking poetry in everyday speech." — LIESEL LITZENBURGER, *Detroit Free Press*

"This engaging collection records both wrenching and riotous episodes in the life of a keenly observant character named Jo Ann, whom we follow from babyhood to marriage and beyond. . . . Humor, terrific insights, and not a little rue make these stories shine, each one a jewel loaded with sparkle and grit." — *Elle*

"Beard pulls off a neat trick: She shows tragedy for what it is in life — plain old moment-to-moment misery." — JANET STEEN, *Time Out New York*

"Exquisitely crafted autobiographical essays that have the arc and thrust of good fiction. . . . Beard's high-wire trick is that despite such grievous subject matter, she hangs on to her squinty, skinny-girl-on-the-sidelines sense of humor and never lapses into mawkishness." — SARAH TOWERS, *Mirabella*

"Jo Ann Beard's work impresses me no end. Funny without being sitcomish, self-aware without being self-absorbed, scrupulous without being fussy, emotional without being sentimental, pointed without being cruel — I could go on and on with these distinctions, all in Beard's favor, but instead I'll just say that Jo Ann Beard is a fantastic writer, an Athena born fully formed out of her own painstaking head." — JEFFREY EUGENIDES, author of *The Virgin Suicides*

The Boys of My Youth

Autobiographical Essays

JO ANN BEARD

BACK BAY BOOKS

LITTLE, BROWN AND COMPANY

New York Boston London

Back Bay Books / Little, Brown and Company
Hachette Book Group
237 Park Avenue, New York, NY 10017
www.hachettebookgroup.com

Originally published in hardcover by Little, Brown and Company, 1998
First Back Bay paperback edition, 1999

Back Bay Books is an imprint of Little, Brown and Company. The Back Bay Books
name and logo are trademarks of Hachette Book Group, Inc.

The publisher is not responsible for websites (or their content)
that are not owned by the publisher.

The events described in these stories are real. Some characters are composites and
some have been given fictitious names and identifying characteristics in order to
protect their anonymity.

"Coyotes" first appeared in *Story;* "Out There" and "Waiting" appeared in *Iowa
Woman;* "Bonanza" appeared in *The Iowa Review;* "Cousins" appeared in *Prairie
Schooner;* and "The Fourth State of Matter" appeared in *The New Yorker.*

The author is grateful for permission to include the following previously
copyrighted material: Excerpts from "Over My Head" by Christine McVie.
Copyright © 1977 by Fleetwood Mac Music (BMI). Reprinted by permission of NEM
Entertainment. Excerpts from "Good Hearted Woman" by Willie Nelson and Waylon
Jennings. Copyright © 1971 by Full Nelson Music, Inc., and Songs of Polygram
International, Inc. All rights on behalf of Full Nelson Music, Inc., administered by
Windswept Pacific Entertainment Co. d/b/a Longitude Music Co. Reprinted by
permission of Full Nelson Music, Inc., and songs of Polygram International, Inc.

LIBRARY OF CONGRESS CATALOGING-IN-PUBLICATION DATA
Beard, Jo Ann.
The boys of my youth / Jo Ann Beard. — 1st ed.
p. cm.
ISBN 978-0-316-08554-0 (hc) / 978-0-316-08525-0 (pb)
1. Beard, Jo Ann. 2. United States — Biography. I. Title.
CT275.B5394A3 1998
973 — dc21
[B]   97-29710

10   9   8   7

RRD-IN

Book design by Julia Sedykh

Printed in the United States of America

for BRAD *and* LINDA   starts @ 3 yr old

jumps in time — example 33-34
                                  36-37
well, all the time

Sounds like poetry P 65

pg 114 sounds diff fr.
              1st chapt even
              tho a kid — diff
              ages?

p. 121
p. 145 husband embarassed
              of her

p. 160
p. 163
              p. 167 38 yrs old

171 — husb's affair
intermit. w H.S.

p 196 — 19th birthday
p 199 — 1976
              feminism strikes

Contents

Acknowledgments

I *would like to express my gratitude* to the Corporation of Yaddo and the MacDowell Colony, for their generous gift of time, and the Constance Saltonstall Foundation in Ithaca, for much-needed financial support. My sincere appreciation to Lizzie Grossman for her sustained belief in my writing, her sanity, and her charming unwillingness to accept rejection when it came our way.

For their friendship, support, and encouragement, I offer profound thanks to Marilyn Abildskov, Mary Allen, Julene Bair, Charlie Buck, Barbara Camillo, Martha Christiansen, Marian Clark, Tory Dent, Sara DiDonato, Ellen Fagg, Gaile Gallatin, Wesley Gibson, Kathy Harris, Tony Hoagland, Will Jennings, Kathy Kiley, Carl Klaus, Edward Lawler, Jane and Michael O'Melia, Maxine Rodburg, Corbin Sexton, Bob Shacochis, Kathy Siebenmann, Jo Southard, David Stern, Patricia Stevens, Shirley Tarbell, and that beloved girl of my youth, Elizabeth White.

Preface

*H*ere's one of my pre-verbal memories: I'm very little and I'm behind bars, like a baby monkey in a cage. My parents have just put me to bed in a room with bright yellow walls. This is fine with me because in my crib there are various companions — the satin edge of my blue blanket, the chewable plastic circle that hangs down almost to mouth level on a piece of green cord, and a boy doll named Hal with blue eyes and lickable hands and feet made of vinyl. At this point in my life, I love Hal and the satin borders of blankets better than I love any of the humans I know. My mother puts Hal up next to my head as soon as I lie down, which is exactly where I don't want him. I smack him in the face.

"You don't want to hurt *Hal*," my mother says sadly. "I thought Hal was your *friend*."

Hal and I have an agreement that he isn't supposed to come up by my pillow; if I want him I'll go down to his end of the crib. My mother snaps off the light and as she does so the night-light is illuminated, a new thing that I've never seen before. The door closes.

I can see the night-light through the bars of my crib. It is a garish depiction of Mary and Joseph and Jesus, although I don't know that then. Jesus is about my age but he looks mean, and the mom and dad are wearing long coats and no shoes. All three of them are staring at me funny. I start crying without taking my eyes off them.

The door opens and when the light goes on the night-light goes off. I stop crying and sit down by Hal while my mother looks at me. She puts the blanket back over me and leaves. Light off, night-light back on. More crying. This time my father comes in and picks me up, walks me around in a circle, puts me back in the crib with Hal, and leaves. When the light goes off and Jesus comes back on I cry again. This time both of them come in to look at me. My mother is smoking a cigarette.

"Don't ask me," she tells my father.

About three more times and they give up. I am left to wail loudly, which I do for a while, until I happen to turn on my side, looking for the bottle of water they had tried to bribe me with. As soon as I turn over the night-light miraculously disappears. The water is warm, just how I like it, and Hal's face is resting against the soles of my feet. I let go of the bottle and wrap the satin border of the blue blanket around my thumb, put the thumb in my mouth, and close my eyes for the night.

I tried to check out that particular memory with my mother when I grew up. I asked her if she remembered a night when I cried and cried, and couldn't be consoled, and they kept coming in and going back out and nothing they did could help me.

"I don't remember any that *weren't* like that," she said, smoking the same cigarette she'd been smoking for thirty years.

So. Here's a recent memory, from two nights ago. I was riding through upstate New York on a dark blue highway, no particular destination. It was cloudy, the air was springy and cool, the dashboard looked like the control panel of a spaceship. Piano music on the tape deck, a charming guy in the driver's seat. I thought to myself, not for the first time in this life, *Everything is perfect; all those things that I always think are so bad really aren't bad at all*. Then I noticed that out my window the clouds had parted, the clear night sky was suddenly visible, and the moon — a garish yellow disk against a dark wall — seemed to be looking at me funny.

The Boys of My Youth

In the Current

*T*he family vacation. *Heat, flies,*
sand, and dirt. My mother sweeps and complains, my father
forever baits hooks and untangles lines. My younger brother
has brought along his imaginary friend, Charcoal, and my
older sister has brought along a real-life majorette by the name
of Nan. My brother continually practices all-star wrestling
moves on poor Charcoal. "I got him in a figure-four leg lock!"
he will call from the ground, propped up on one elbow, his legs
twisted together. My sister and Nan wear leg makeup, white
lipstick, and say things about me in French. A river runs in
front of our cabin, the color of bourbon, foamy at the banks,
full of water moccasins and doomed fish. I am ten. The only
thing to do is sit on the dock and read, drink watered-down
Pepsi, and squint. No swimming allowed.

One afternoon three teenagers get caught in the current

while I watch. They come sweeping downstream, hollering and gurgling while I stand on the bank, forbidden to step into the water, and stare at them. They are waving their arms.

I am embarrassed because teenagers are yelling at me. Within five seconds men are throwing off their shoes and diving from the dock; my own dad gets hold of one girl and swims her back in. Black hair plastered to her neck, she throws up on the mud about eight times before they carry her back to wherever she came from. One teenager is unconscious when they drag him out and a guy pushes on his chest until a low fountain of water springs up out of his mouth and nose. That kid eventually walks away on his own, but he's crying. The third teenager lands a ways down the bank and comes walking by fifteen minutes later, a grown-up on either side of him and a towel around his waist. His skin looks like Silly Putty.

"Oh man," he says when he sees me. "I saw her go by about ninety miles an hour!" He stops and points at me. I just stand there, embarrassed to be noticed by a teenager. I hope my shorts aren't bagging out again. I put one hand in my pocket and slouch sideways a little. "Man, I thought she was gonna be the last thing I ever seen!" he says, shaking his head.

The girl teenager had had on a swimming suit top with a built-in bra. I cross my arms nonchalantly across my chest and smile at the teenage boy. He keeps walking and talking, the grown-ups supporting him and giving each other looks over the top of his head. His legs are shaking like crazy. "I thought, Man oh man, that skinny little chick is gonna be the last thing *ever*," he exclaims.

I look down. My shorts are bagging out.

Bonanza

M_y *grandmother married a* guy named Ralph, about a year and a half after Pokey, my real grandfather, died of a stroke in the upstairs bedroom of Uncle Rex's house. At Grandma and Ralph's wedding ceremony a man sang opera-style, which took the children by surprise and caused an uproar among the grandchildren, who were barely able to sit still as it was. Afterward, there was white cake with white frosting in the church basement, and bowls of peanuts. My mother and my aunts were quite upset about Grandma marrying Ralph barely a year after their dad had died. They sat in clumps in the church basement, a few here, a few there, and ate their cake while giving each other meaningful looks, shaking their heads ominously. My grandmother, a kind woman, was way above reproach. So, it was all Ralph's fault.

He took her to Florida on a honeymoon, a place where no

one in the family had ever been. There was an ocean there. They walked the beach morning and night, and Grandma brought home shells. She divided them up evenly, put them in cigar boxes, and gave them to each of her thirty-five grandchildren. The cigar boxes were painted flat white and glued to the top were pictures cut from greeting cards: a lamb, a big-eyed kitty, a bunch of flowers. On that trip to Florida, I always imagine my grandmother walking in the foamy tide, picking up dead starfish, while Ralph sat silently in a beach chair, not smiling at anyone.

When we'd drive down to Knoxville for a visit, everyone would be hale and hearty, the food eaten, the iced tea drunk, the new rag rugs admired, and then we'd pile back into the car for the hour ride home. Ralph was always grouchy and harsh, with big fingers that he pointed at everyone while he talked. As soon as we pulled out of the driveway, my mother would look at my father and say, "That old sonuvabitch, I'd like to *kill* him."

I went to visit Grandma and Ralph for a week right after having learned how to whistle. I whistled at all times, with dedication and complete concentration. When I was asked a question I whistled the answer, I whistled along with people as they talked, I whistled while I worked, I whistled while I played. Eventually they made a rule that whistling was forbidden in their house. I felt bereft and didn't know what to do with my lips if I couldn't whistle. I would blow gently, without making a sound, while helping my grandmother get dinner. She must have felt sorry for me because she said once, kindly, "Honey, you *can* whistle when you're outside." But that was no comfort to me. Part of the joy of whistling was knowing that it was always available, you carried the equipment right on your own face. If I couldn't whistle *at all times*, then I didn't care to whistle outdoors. I couldn't wait to get home, where no one could make me do anything.

Grandma and Ralph both worked, so when I went to visit I had hours and hours each day to occupy myself. Grandma took care of senior citizens, some of them younger than she was, shut-ins and disabled folk who needed company and assistance with some of the necessities — cooking, talking. She was a volunteer. Ralph was a butcher and a sheepshearer. He drove a panel truck out to people's farms and killed their cattle for them. Eyes like pebbles, tanned face pulled into a knotty smile, bald head glinting in the sun, a foot-long knife blade aimed at unsuspecting furred throats. Afterward he would use a garden hose to spray out the back of his truck. White walls and floor, pools and spatters of brilliant red. I glimpsed it once, without knowing what I was looking at. I remember thinking, "That looks like *blood*." It never occurred to me it *was* blood. The sheep, after being sheared, stood stunned, in masses, their sides heaving, long cuts and gashes on their pink, exposed skin. The wool stank like crazy and lay in mounds everywhere, gray and filthy. I was taken along on his sprees, sent off to play with complete strangers, farm children, while he went to work with his long knife, his buzzing clippers. I was known for being sensitive to the plight of farm animals and bunnies killed on the road, but I steadfastly refused to acknowledge what was taking place on those visits. I never figured out what was going on around me, even when it was written on the walls in red.

I went along with Grandma sometimes, too. I saw a lady who slept in a crib, curled like a four-year-old, so tiny. She stared out from the bars at me with blank blue eyes. My grandma helped her husband turn her over. Their living room smelled like pee and something else. We had a covered dish for the husband in our trunk and I carried it in. The old woman had white hair that stuck up in patches on her head. I couldn't get over that she slept in a crib, and I couldn't stop looking at her. My grandma called out to her before we left. "Eva!" she called, "we brung Walter your noodle ring! But it don't taste nothing like what you made; I didn't have pumpernickel so I used white!" The words of grown-ups rarely made real sense to me. But Eva understood, and smiled faintly at us, her blue eyes staring through the bars.

"Oh, I got her smilin'," my grandma crowed. Walter walked us out to the car and stood while we drove away, a wide man in overalls and a pressed shirt. He waved to us by touching his temple gently with two fingers, and then pointing them at us. I waved back at him that way.

But mostly I stayed behind, at their house, and wandered through the rooms, picking things up and putting them back down. There were unimaginable treasures there, old things that you didn't know the purpose of, beautiful spindly-legged furniture, and things with exotic, lost names. Chifforobes and highboys, antimacassars and lowboys. Every surface of every wall was covered, and nearly every inch of floor space was, too. Only in the middle of each room was a cleared space for living, a more or less empty zone. Jars of buttons, every kind imaginable, homemade ones, bone ones, small pink and white ones ("Them're for a baby's dress," she told me), enormous black ones. They were endlessly fascinating to me, all their colors and textures, the satisfying *churrr* as they poured out of the jar and onto a table. I didn't quite know what to do with them then; they seemed to call out for some special kind of play, something that would lend itself to a pile of buttons. But I could never think of what to do with them next, so I would put them back in the jar, put the jar back on the table or shelf or closet that it had come out of, and wander on to the next thing. A small drawer in a small dresser, long thin tools with carved handles, a whole bunch of them rubber-banded together. "Them're buttonhooks," she told me, "from when you had buttons on your shoes." I didn't know what she was talking about, and set them back in their small drawer, closed it. On almost every surface there was an antique vase with a bouquet of flowers in it, set in the middle of a starched doily. Beautiful, exotic blooms, all plastic, all covered with a heavy layer of dust. "They throw 'em away, just like they didn't cost money," my grandma would explain.

I spent long days of blistering, stupefying boredom in that house, opening the refrigerator and staring into it forty times in an afternoon. Butter, milk, bowls with clumped food visible through their Saran Wrapped tops. There was stuff to eat to make you go to the bathroom, stuff to drink to make you go to the bathroom, and then several things to make you *stop* going to the bathroom. Nothing sweet whatsoever. She'd make a batch of cookies before I came and put them in the fat-chef cookie jar. I would eat all the cookies on the first morning, and then hunt relentlessly the rest of the week for something sweet. I would remember the cookies — greasy peanut butter ones with peanuts stuck in them, or chocolate chip ones with oatmeal — with a kind of hysterical longing. I couldn't believe I had eaten every one of them the first morning. What could I have been thinking?

I ate sugar cubes from the sugar bowl, one every hour or so. They were actually *too* sugary and each time I ate one I swore I wouldn't do it again. But another hour later would find me creeping sock-footed out to the kitchen, lifting the plastic lid of the sugar bowl, and selecting another.

Sometimes I would jump energetically on the beds, two twin ones that were in the room where I slept. I'd kung fu all the embroidered throw pillows onto the floor, and then jump and jump and jump, saying a Chinese jump-rope chant: "Chicka-chicka China, sitting on a fence, tried to make a dollar outta fifty-nine cents," until I was so out of breath I had to collapse on my back and wait for the rotating fan to turn in my direction.

Oh, the rotating fan.

The lovely rotating fan, something that moved of its own accord in the dead house during the long afternoons. I would set the rotating fan on a footstool in the long, narrow bedroom. My job was to feed Kleenexes into it and then pick up the shredded pieces. By the end of one of those stultifying afternoons, I'd have an empty Kleenex box and a whole wastebasket full of soft pink confetti. Nobody ever questioned where the Kleenexes went when I was visiting, but once my grandma gave me another white-painted cigar box that was full of handkerchiefs, neatly pressed and folded. Every kind imaginable: flowered, embroidered, ones with Scottie terriers, ones with lace edges, the whole bit.

They ate terrible food, things mixed together that weren't supposed to be. Mashed potatoes with corn, pieces of white bread with gravy poured on top, peas and carrots in the same bowl. Ralph would have a dish towel tucked into his collar and hold a fork and spoon in his enormous paws. He'd get something on the spoon, a great gob of potatoes, say, and then open his mouth as wide as it would go, like a bird in a nest getting fed a chewed worm. He had deep creases on either side of his mouth, and as he chewed, gravy would run down the gullies in rivulets, land on the dish towel, and stay there. It was an amazing and horrifying thing to watch. I had a sensitive stomach and sometimes, sitting across from him — eyes carefully averted, fastened on the Aunt Jemima potholder hanging on a hook or on a pan lid with a screw and a block of wood jimmied up for a handle — just hearing him eat could make me gag. I was in the habit of rising from the table and walking around the kitchen every few minutes, breathing through my nose, deeply, to keep from gagging. Then I'd sit back down, pick up two peas with my spoon, and put them in my mouth. This is what my grandma said to me once: "Eat your chicken, why don't you? And don't take the skin off, that's what's good."

They were trying to make me eat something with *skin* on it. At my own house, everyone knew enough not to say *skin* in relation to food.

My grandma, when she was cooking dinner, would send me down to the fruit cellar for jars of home-canned stuff. Then when I'd bring them up she'd open the jars and smell the contents thoughtfully; sometimes she'd have me take the jar outside to where Ralph was and have him smell it. He always said the same things: "There ain't nothing wrong with *that*, tell her" or he'd bawl toward the house as I was walking back in, "Maw, that'll be okay if you cook it longer!"

Once she served me red raspberries that she'd put up; poured them in a plastic bowl and put cream on them. As I started to dig in I noticed that there were some black things floating around. "Grandma, there's bugs in this," I said. She came over and looked into my bowl, head tipped back to see out of the bottoms of her glasses. "Them're dead," she told me. "Just push 'em to the side; the berries is okay." And I did, and the berries *were* okay.

At night we watched one show on TV and then had to go to bed, when it was still a little bit light out. They'd go in their room and my grandma would come out with her nightgown on and her teeth out to tuck me in. I'd be lying stiff as a plank under the bedspread and here she'd come, without her regular clothes on, with her arms and feet exposed, her mouth folded in on itself. "G'night, honey-Jo," she would lisp, pat me on the shoulder, and turn out the light. And there I'd be, while they snored up one side and down the other in the room across the hall. I'd tiptoe all over the bedroom, gazing for a while out the window, watching the sky turn black, the stars come out. I'd quietly open all the drawers of all the dressers in the room, take out things, examine them, put them back. I didn't dare jump on the bed, although sometimes I said "Chicka-chicka China" to myself out of boredom. I tried counting sheep like on the cartoons, but I couldn't concentrate, couldn't for the life of me imagine what sheep looked like. I knew but I didn't know, just as I couldn't conjure up the faces of my long-lost parents and siblings. I was wide-awake, staring out at the vast Milky Way while the grown-ups snored on and on and the moon rose and sank.

The strange thing was, I always asked to go there. I don't remember them ever inviting me, or my parents suggesting it. It was me. From far away the idea of their house was magical to me, all those nooks, all those crannies, all those things to play with — the button jars, the lowboy with a little drawer full of marbles, the flower arrangements, the rotating fan. So, every July I got dropped off on a Sunday and picked up the following Sunday. By Tuesday I'd be counting the hours, sitting on the backyard glider, staring at the black lawn jockey and the flagstone path that took you to the garden, the broken bird bath with a pool of rusty, skanky water in it. Their yard had as much stuff in it as their house did, only the yard stuff was filthy, full of dirt and rainwater.

The last time I went there my parents drove off on a Sunday afternoon as I stood on the gravel sidewalk and waved, already regretting my visit. My grandma fed us, dinner was the usual ordeal of gravy rivulets and tainted food, and then they turned *Bonanza* on. I lay on the living room floor, in the cleared-out space in the center; on either end of the couch were Grandma and Ralph. She was knitting an afghan and he was sharpening a stack of scissors.

We were watching my favorite show. The dad, Ben, had a buckskin, Hoss had a black horse, and Little Joe had a pinto pony. They had Hop Sing for a servant, in place of a mom. Back home my little brother would be humming to himself through the whole show, "Umbuddy-umbuddy-umbuddy-ummm Bonanza," and everyone would be telling him to shut up. My mom would be smoking her cigarettes and drinking beer out of a bottle, my dad would have his socks off and be stretching his bare toes, drinking his beer out of a glass. My sister would be trying to do homework at the dining room table.

Here I was with Grandma and Ralph, staying up one hour later than I would the rest of the century-long week. Little Joe falls in love with a schoolteacher who comes past the Ponderosa in a buggy. He kisses her a long one, it stretches out forever in the silence of the living room. There isn't a sound from behind me, on the couch. No one is moving while the kiss is going on. It's horrible. I look around the room, at the pictures that cover every inch of wall space, my aunts and uncles and their families, framed sayings from the olden days, plaques with jokes about outhouses, a pair of flying ceramic ducks with orange beaks and feet, and on and on. Too much to look at. The pecking-hen salt and pepper shakers, the donkey with a dead plant coming out of his back, the stacks of old magazines under tables and on the seats of chairs. Underneath me are three scatter rugs, converging their corners in a lump under my back. Rag rugs, one of them made from bread wrappers. Hoss Cartwright saves the schoolteacher when her horse shies and now she's in love with him. Little Joe tries to punch Hoss out. Behind me my grandmother's knitting needles click together in a sad and empty way, Ralph's breathing is audible over the scratch of scissor blades on stone. In the dim circle of light that I lay in, my head cushioned on an Arkansas Razorback pillow, I feel completely separate from them because of the simple fact that in seven days I will be rescued, removed from this terrible lonely place and put back in the noisy house I came from.

It occurs to me that Grandma and Ralph have nothing, they don't even enjoy *Bonanza* all that much, they just turned it on because my mom told them to let me watch it. There can't be anything for them to enjoy, with their long empty days, full of curled-up old ladies and dirty sheep. They don't even drink pop.

I am crying on the floor, the tears go sideways and land coldly in my ears or on the velveteen pillow. I can't bear, suddenly, the way the television sends out its sad blue light, making the edges of the room seem darker. A coffee can covered with contact paper holds red, white, and blue Fourth of July flowers, taken from a dead person. I wish suddenly that my grandma was dead, so she wouldn't have to knit that afghan anymore. The rest of the year, while I'm gone back home and am playing with my friends, this is where my grandma is, her needles going, her teeth in the bathroom in a plastic bowl. My ears are swimming pools, and I feel trapped suddenly inside the small circle of light in the center of the room. I'm tiny Eva, watching Little Joe Cartwright through the bars of my crib, I'm a monkey, strapped into a space capsule and flung far out into the galaxy, weightless, hurtling along upside down through the Milky Way. Alone, alone, and alone. Against my will, I sob out loud. I turn over and weep into the Arkansas pillow, wrecking the velveteen. Suddenly my grandma's hand is on my hair, the knitting needles have been set down.

There is telephone talk, and muffled comments from Grandma to Ralph, from Ralph to the person on the other end of the phone. My nose is pressed against the pillow and I'm still crying, or trying to. I suddenly want to hear what's going on but I don't have the nerve to sit up. My clothes are gathered, the television is shut off, I am walked outside and put in the back seat of their great big yellow car. In the back window, there's a dog with a bobbing head that I usually like to mess around with when I'm riding in the car. I don't even bother to look at it; I just stare out the back window at the night sky.

After about a half hour of driving we pull over and sit at the side of the road. I'm no longer weightless, but unbearably heavy, and tired. My dad pulls up with a crunch of gravel, words are exchanged through open windows, quiet chuckles, I am placed in the front seat between my parents. We pull away, and as we head toward home, the galaxy recedes, the stars move back into position, and the sky stretches out overhead, black and familiar.

They've decided not to hassle me about this. "What happened, honey?" my mom asks once, gently.

"*Bonanza* made me sad," I reply.

Cousins

*H*ere is a scene. Two sisters are fishing together in a flat-bottomed boat on an olive green lake. They sit slumped like men, facing in opposite directions, drinking coffee out of a metal-sided thermos, smoking intently. Without their lipstick they look strangely weary, and passive, like pale replicas of their real selves. They both have a touch of morning sickness but neither is admitting it. Instead, they watch their bobbers and argue about worms versus minnows.

My cousin and I are floating in separate, saline oceans. I'm the size of a cocktail shrimp and she's the size of a man's thumb. My mother is the one on the left, wearing baggy gabardine trousers and a man's shirt. My cousin's mother is wearing blue jeans, cuffed at the bottom, and a cotton blouse printed with wild cowboys roping steers. Their voices carry, as usual, but at this point we can't hear them.

It is five A.M. A duck stands up, shakes out its feathers, and peers above the still grass at the edge of the water. The skin of the lake twitches suddenly and a fish springs loose into the air, drops back down with a flat splash. Ripples move across the surface like radio waves. The sun hoists itself up and gets busy, laying a sparkling rug across the water, burning the beads of dew off the reeds, baking the tops of our mothers' heads. One puts on sunglasses and the other a plaid fishing cap with a wide brim.

In the cold dark underwater, a long fish with a tattered tail discovers something interesting. He circles once and then has his breakfast before becoming theirs. As he breaks from the water to the air he twists hard, sending out a cold spray, sparks of green light. My aunt reels him in, triumphant, and grins at her sister, big teeth in a friendly mouth.

"Why you dirty rotten so-and-so," my mother says admiringly.

It is nine o'clock on Saturday night, the sky is black and glittering with pinholes, old trees are bent down over the highway. In the dark field behind, the corn gathers its strength, grows an inch in the silence, then stops to rest. Next to the highway, screened in vegetation, a deer with muscular ears and glamorous eyes stands waiting to spring out from the wings into the next moving spotlight. The asphalt sighs in anticipation.

The car is a late-model Firebird, black on black with a T-roof and a tape deck that pelts out anguish, Fleetwood Mac. My cousin looks just like me except she has coarse hair and the jawline of an angel. She's driving and I'm shotgun, talking to her profile. The story I'm recounting to her is full of what I said back to people when they said things to me. She can sing and listen at the same time, so she does that, nodding and grimacing when necessary.

She interrupts me once. "What's my hair doing?"

"Laying down. I'll tell you if it tries anything." Her hair is short but so dense it has a tendency to stay wherever the wind pushes it. When she wakes up in the morning her head is like a landscape, with cliffs and valleys, spectacular pinnacles.

"Okay, go ahead," she says. I finish my story before my favorite song comes on so I can devote myself to it.

We sing along to a tune about a woman who rings like a bell through the night. Neither of us knows what that means, but we're in favor of it. We want to ring like bells, we want our hair to act right, we want to go out with guys who wear boots with turned-up toes and worn-down heels. We're out in the country, on my cousin's turf. My car is stalled in the city somewhere on four low tires, a blue-and-rust Volkswagen with the door coat-hangered shut. Her car is this streamlined, dark-eyed Firebird with its back end hiked up like a skirt. We are hurtling through the night, as they say, on our way to a bar where the guys own speedboats, snowmobiles, whatever else is current. I sing full-throttle: *You can take me to paradise, but then again you can be cold as ice; I'm over my head, but it sure feels nice.* I turn the rearview mirror around, check to see what's happening with the face.

Nothing good. But there you have it. It's yours at least, and your hair isn't liable to thrust itself upward into stray pointing fingers. It doesn't sound like corn husks when you brush it.

My cousin, beautiful in the dashboard light, glances over at me. She has a first name but I've always called her Wendell. She pushes it up to eighty and the song ends, a less wonderful one comes on. We're coming to the spot on the highway where the giant trees dangle their wrists over the ground. In the crotch of an elm, during daylight hours, a gnarled car is visible, wedged among the branches.

Up ahead, the cornfields are dark and rustling. The deer shifts nervously behind the curtain of weeds, waiting for its cue. The car in the tree's crotch is a warning to fast drivers, careening kids. Hidden beneath the driver's seat, way up in the branches, is a silver pocketwatch with a broken face. It had been someone's great-grandfather's, handed down and handed down, until it reached the boy who drove his car into the side of a tree. Below the drifting branches, the ground is black and loamy, moving with bugs. In the silence, stalks of corn stretch their thin, thready feet and gather in the moisture. The pocketwatch is stopped at precisely 11:47, as was the boy. Fleetwood Mac rolls around the bend and the deer springs full-blown out of the brocade trees. In the white pool of headlights, in front of a swerving audience, it does a short, stark, modern dance, and exits to the right. We recover and slow it down, shaking.

"He could have wrecked my whole front end," Wendell says. This is the farm-kid mentality. Her idea of a gorgeous deer is one that hangs upside down on the wall of the shed, a rib cage, a pair of antlers, a gamy hunk of dinner. She feels the same way about cows and pigs.

We're in the sticks. Way out here things are measured in shitloads, and every third guy you meet is named Junior. I've decided I don't even like this bar we're going to, that howling three-man band and the bathroom with no stalls, just stools. Now I'm slumped and surly, an old pose for me. That deer had legs like canes, feet like Dixie cups.

Wendell pats my knee, grinning. "Settle down," she says. "It didn't *hit* us. We're safe." She likes excitement as long as her car doesn't get hurt. I light a cigarette, begin dirtying up her ashtray, and mess with the tape until our favorite song comes on again. We're back up to eighty on the narrow highway, daring the ignorant to take a step onto the asphalt. This is Illinois, a land of lumbering raccoons, snake-tailed possums, and flat-out running bunnies, all trying to cross the road. The interior of the car smells like leather and evergreen trees, the moon peers through the roof, and Wendell drives with one finger.

"Hey, how's my hair?" she asks suddenly. Her eyes are clear brown, her cheekbones are high and delicate, brushed with pink, her lips aren't too big or too little. She's wearing my shirt. A clump of hair has pushed itself forward in the excitement. It looks like a small, startled hand rising from the back of her head.

I make an okay sign, thumb and forefinger. The music is deafening.

Back in the cluster of trees, the deer moves into position again and the willows run their fingers along the ground. The corn whispers encouragement to itself. In the bar up ahead waitresses slam sloe-gin fizzes down on wet tables and men point pool cues at each other in the early stages of drunkenness. The singer in the three-man band whispers *test* into the microphone and rolls his eyes at the feedback. The sound guy jumps up from a table full of ladies and heads over to turn knobs.

We crunch over the parking lot gravel and wait for our song to finish. *I'm over my head, but it sure feels nice.* The bar is low and windowless, with patched siding and a kicked-in door; the lot is full of muscle cars and pickups. A man and a woman burst through the door and stand negotiating who will drive. He's got the keys but she looks fiercer. In the blinking neon our faces are malarial and buttery. As the song winds down, the drama in front of us ends. He throws the keys at her as hard as he can but she jumps nimbly out of the way and picks them up with a handful of gravel, begins pelting his back as he weaves into the darkness.

Wendell turns to me with a grin, a question on her lips. Before she can ask I reach over and press her excited hair back down.

Their house has a face on it, two windows with the shades half
down, a brown slot of a door, and a glaring mouthful of railing
with a few pickets missing. Pink geraniums grow like earrings
on either side of the porch. It's August and the grass is golden
and spiky against our ankles, the geraniums smell like dust. A
row of hollyhocks stands out by the road, the flowers are
upside-down ladies, red, maroon, and dried-up brown. An exploded raccoon is abuzz over on the far side of the highway and
crows are dropping down from time to time to sort among the
pieces. On either side of the house, fields fall away, rolling and
baking in the heat.

The sisters are sitting on the stoop shelling peas, talking
overtop of each other. My mother says mayonnaise goes bad in
two hours in the hot sun and my aunt says bullshit. They've
just driven out to the fields and left the lunches for the hired
men. They argue energetically about this, until the rooster
walks up and my aunt carries her bowl in the house to finish
the discussion through the screen door. She and the rooster
hate each other.

"He thinks you're a chicken," my mother explains. "You
have to show him you won't put up with it." She picks up a
stick, threatens the rooster with it, and he backs off, pretends
to peck the yard. My aunt comes back out.

The front of her head is in curlers, the brush kind that hurt,
and she keeps testing her hair to see if it's done. She has on a
smock with big pockets and pedal pushers. Her feet are bare,
one reason why the rooster is scaring her so much. My mother
doesn't wear curlers because her hair is short but she has two
clips crisscrossed on either side of her head, making spit curls
in front of her ears. Every time a car drives by she reaches up
automatically, ready to yank them out. She has on Bermuda

shorts and a wide-bottomed plaid blouse with a bow at the neck. They are both pregnant again.

We're going to be in a parade at four o'clock, Wendell and I, riding bikes without training wheels, our dolls in the baskets. We asked to have the training wheels put back on for the parade but they said no. Our older sisters are upstairs somewhere, dumping perfume on one another and trying on bracelets. They'll be in the parade, too, walking behind us and throwing their batons in the air, trying to drop them on our heads.

Wendell jumps at the rooster suddenly and he rushes us, we go off screaming in different directions while he stands there furious, shifting from one scaly foot to another, slim and tall with greasy black feathers and a yellow ruff like a collie. He can make the dirty feathers around his neck stand up and fall back down whenever he gets mad, just like flexing a muscle. Even his wives give him a wide berth, rolling their seedy eyes and murmuring. They get no rest. I haven't yet connected the chickens walking around out here with what we had for lunch, chopped up and mixed with mayonnaise.

The mothers give up and go in the house to smoke cigarettes at the kitchen table and yell at us through the windows. Wendell and I work on decorating our bikes and complaining about no training wheels.

"What about if there's a *corner*?" I say.

"I know," says Wendell. "Or if there's *dog* poop?" I don't know exactly how this relates but I shudder anyway. We shake our heads and try twisting the crepe paper into the spokes the way our mothers showed us but it doesn't work. We end up with gnarled messes and flounce into the house to discipline our dolls.

Here is the parade. Boys in cowboy getups with cap guns and rubber spurs, hats that hang from shoestrings around their necks. The girls squint against the sun and press their stiff dresses down. This is the year of the can-can slip so we all have on good underpants without holes. Some kids have their ponies there, ornery things with rolling eyes and bared teeth, all decorated up. Two older boys with painted-on mustaches beat wildly on drums until they are stopped. Mothers spit on Kleenexes and go at the boys' faces while fathers stand around comparing what their watches say to what the sun is doing.

Two little girls wear matching dresses made from a big linen tablecloth, a white background with blue and red fruit clusters. One has a bushy stand of hair and the other a smooth pixie. Both have large bows, one crunched into the mass and the other practically taped on. The scalloped collars on their dresses are made from the border of the tablecloth, bright red with tiny blue grapes, little green stems. There are sashes tied in perfect bows, and pop-bead bracelets. Our shoes don't match.

The dolls rode over to the parade in the trunk of the car so we wouldn't wreck their outfits. They have the ability to drink water and pee it back out but they're dry now, our mothers put a stop to that. They have on dresses to match ours, with tiny scalloped collars and ribbon sashes. We set them carefully in our bike baskets with their skirts in full view. Mine's hair is messed up on one side where I put hairspray on it once. Wendell's has a chewed-up hand and nobody knows how it got that way. We stand next to our crepe-papered bikes in the sunlight, waiting for them to tell us what to do.

Our sisters have been forbidden to throw their batons until the parade starts and so they twirl them around and pretend to hurl them up in the air, give a little hop, and pretend to catch them again. They are wearing perfume and fingernail polish with their cowboy boots and shorts. They don't like us very much but we don't care.

My mother tells me to stand up straight and Wendell's mother tells her to push her hair back down. The baton twirlers get a last minute talking-to with threats. The parade moves out ragged and wobbly, someone immediately starts crying, a pony wanders out of line and looks for some grass to chew. The main street is crowded with bystanders and parked automobiles. It is never clear what this parade is for, except to dress the children up and show them off, get the men to come in from the fields for a while.

As the parade pulls itself slowly down the street, the mothers stand with wry, proud faces and folded arms while fathers stand smoking, lifting the one-finger farmer's salute as their sons go by. Wendell and I steer carefully and watch our mothers as they move along the sidewalk, following. Tall, lanky frames and watermelon stomachs, the gray eyes and beautiful hands of the Patterson side of the family. Our dolls are behaving perfectly, staring straight ahead, slumped forward in their baskets. My sash has come untied and Wendell's underpants are showing. We don't care, they won't bother fixing us now; we're in the parade and they have to stay on the sidewalk.

The street is brilliant in the sun, and the children move in slow motion, dresses, cowboy hats, tap shoes, the long yellow teeth of the mean ponies. At the count of four, one of our sisters loses control, throws her baton high in the air and stops, one hand out to catch it when it comes back down.

For a long, gleaming moment it hangs there, a silver hyphen against the hot sky. Over the hectic heads of the children and the smooth blue-and-white blur of crepe-papered spokes and handlebar streamers, above the squinting smiles and upturned eyes, a silver baton rises miraculously, lingers for a moment against the sun, and then drops back down, into the waiting hand.

Back at the bar, someone has hold of me and I'm on the dance floor. Wendell's standing just inside the door. I'm going backward swiftly, in a fast two-step, there's an arm slung across my shoulder. It's good old Ted, trying to make a girl feel welcome. The bar is as dark as a pocket and my eyes haven't adjusted yet. Ted runs me into a couple of people and I tell him his arm weighs a ton. He grins but doesn't move it. He has long legs and a drinking problem. Two ex-wives follow him everywhere, stirring up trouble.

When the song finally ends, I untangle from Ted and look for Wendell. She's got us a table back by the wall, beneath the bored head of a deer. As I pass the bar several guys in turn swivel their stools around and catch me. Blue-jeaned legs are parted, I'm pulled in, pressed against a chest, clamped. Hello, hello. I bum a cigarette from the first one and blow smoke in the face of the second when his hand crawls like a bull snake up the back of my shirt. Even way out here I'm known for being not that easy to get along with.

Wendell takes her feet off my chair and pushes a rum and Pepsi my way. She tries to tell me something over the din.

"What?" I holler back and turn my ear to her.

"I *said*, your *buddy*'s here," she yells into my hair. I pull back and look at her. She jerks a thumb upward, to the passive, suspended face of the deer. Someone has stuck a cigarette butt in one of its nostrils. I show her my middle finger and she sits back again, satisfied. Side by side at the spindly table, we drink our drinks for a while and watch the dancers go around.

Ida's out there, going to town, seventy-five if she's a day, with dyed black hair and tall, permanently arched eyebrows. From nine to midnight, even when it's just the jukebox, she takes herself around the dance floor — fox-trot, swing shuffle, two-step. She comes here every Saturday night to dance by herself while her grandson drinks Mountain Dew and plays pool in the back room. Her tennis shoes look like they're disconnected from the rest of her body. Every once in a while, she presses one hand against her waist and closes her eyes for an instant, keeping time with her shoulders, all part of some interior dancing-drama, some memory of Pete and her, before they got old, before she up and got widowed. Apparently, they were quite a deal on the dance floor. Nobody ever bumps into her out there, even the drunkest of the drunk make a space for those shoes and that head of hair. She's dancing with a memory, putting all the rest of us to shame.

Here comes our darling Nick. Everyone's in love with him, blond hair in a ponytail and wire-rims, drives a muddy jeep. Too bad he's related to us. He sets us up with two more drinks, takes a joint out of his shirt pocket, puts it in my cigarette pack, and lays a big kiss on Wendell, flat on the lips. Right as he leaves, he zooms in on me unexpectedly. I give him one hand to shake and put the other one over my mouth. Wendell takes a drink and leans over.

"Gross," she shouts into my ear. I nod. Cousin cooties.

"I'm telling Aunt Bernie," I shout back. Aunt Bernie is his mom.

We've been sitting too long. Wendell carries her drink, I light a cigarette, and we move out into the revelers, and lose each other. The rum is a warm, dark curtain in my chest. I suddenly look better than I have in weeks, I can feel geraniums blooming in my cheeks, my mouth is genuinely smiling for once, my hair, fresh from the ironing board, falls like a smooth plank down my back. It's Saturday night and I'm three rum and Pepsis to the wind. I love this bar, the floor is a velvet trampoline, a mirrored ball revolves above the dance floor, stars move across faces and hands, everyone encountered is a close personal friend. I'm in line for the bathroom, chatting with strangers.

"I like your shirt." This from the woman behind me, she may be trying to negotiate her way up the line.

"Thanks," I tell her. She's pretty. "I like yours, too."

"Your cousin's really drunk," she says, rolling her eyes. I guess she knows me. She means Nick, not Wendell. Women are always striking up conversations about Nick.

"I know" is what I tell her. I smile when I say it and shrug, trying to indicate that she can come to family dinners with Nick as far as I'm concerned. We lapse back into silence until the door bursts open and three women come out, reeking of reefer and perfume.

I look at the woman who struck up the conversation with me. We raise our eyebrows.

"Nice perfume," she says, wrinkling her nose.

"Nice reefer," I say. I let her come in while I go and she checks her makeup and examines her teeth in the mirror. I wait for her, too, bending over at the waist, shaking the hair out, and then flipping it back. It makes it fluffier for a few minutes, before it settles back into the plank again. The bending and flipping sends the room careening for a moment, I'm in a centrifugal tube, then it halts. She wants to know who Nick's going out with.

"His dog, I think," I tell her. I'm politely not noticing her peeing. "He's got the nicest golden retriever you ever saw." I love that dog; it refuses to hunt, just walks along and stirs up ducks and pheasants, watches with surprise when they go flapping off. "That's one thing about Nick. His dog's nice." I don't think Nick ever shoots anything anyway, he just looks good in the boots and the vest.

Actually, I think Cousin Nick's going out with everyone, but I don't tell her that. She looks hopeful and sparkly and she's not nearly as drunk as me. I give her a swimmy smile on the way out and we part company forever.

The band rolls into a slow one, with a creaky metallic guitar hook and a lone warbling voice. Someone asks me to dance and we stroll around the floor, amid the stars and the elbows. I close my eyes for a moment and it's night inside my head, there are strange arms moving me around, this way and that, feet bumping into mine. The steel guitar comes overtop of it all, climbing and dropping, locating everyone's sadness and yanking on it. In the shuffling crowd the dark curtain of rum parts for an instant, and reveals nothing. I open my eyes and look up at my partner. He's leading away, a grinning stranger, his hand strolls down and finds my back pocket, warms itself. Christ Almighty.

Ida swims through, and past, eyes blank as nickels, disembodied feet, arms like floating strings. One song ends and a new one starts up, I shake my head at my partner and he backs off with a sullen shrug. Apparently he likes this song because he begins fast-dancing by himself, looking hopefully around at the other dancers, trying to rope a stray.

This is Wendell's favorite song, *She's a good-hearted wo-man, in love with a two-timing man.* Here she is, ready to dance. I move with her back into the lumbering crowd on the dance floor, and we carve out a little spot in front of the band. *She loves him in spite of his wicked ways she don't understand.* The bar has gone friendly again while I wasn't looking, the faces of the other dancers are pink with exertion and alcohol, Nick's dancing with the bathroom girl, Ted's twirling an ex-wife, the singer in the band knocks the spit out of his harmonica and attaches it to his neck again. Look at Wendell's face. She's twenty-one and single; her hair has a story to tell. In the small sticky space in front of the band, we twirl a few times, knuckles and lifted elbows, under and over, until I get stomped on. We're singing now, recklessly, it's almost closing time and us girls are getting prettier by the moment. *Through teardrops and laughter we pass through this world hand in hand.* Of course, both Wendell and I would like to be good-hearted women but we're from the Patterson clan, and just don't have the temperament for it.

The sisters are making deviled eggs. They have on dark blue dresses with aprons and are walking around in nyloned feet. No one can find the red stuff that gets sprinkled on top of the eggs. They're tearing the cupboards apart right now, swearing to each other and shaking their heads. We all know enough to stay out of the kitchen.

We're at my grandma's house in our best dresses with towels pinned to the collars. Our older sisters are walking around with theatrical, mournful faces, bossing us like crazy, in loud disgusted whispers. They have their pockets loaded with Kleenex in preparation for making a scene. We're all going to our grandfather's funeral in fifteen minutes, as soon as the paprika gets found.

Wendell and I get to go only because we promised to act decent. No more running and sliding on the funeral-home rug. Someone has *died*, and there's a time and a place for everything. We'll both get spanked in front of everyone and put in chairs if we're not careful. And if we can't keep our gum in our mouths then we don't need it: both pieces are deposited in a held-out Kleenex on the ride over. Wendell and I are in disgrace from our behavior last night at the visitation.

"It wasn't our fault he moved," Wendell had explained, right before being swatted in the funeral-home foyer. Our grandfather had looked like a big, dead doll in a satin doll bed. We couldn't stop staring, and then suddenly, simultaneously, got spooked and ran out of the room, squealing and holding on to each other. We stayed in the foyer for the rest of the night, greeting people and taking turns sliding the rug across the glossy floor. We were a mess by the end of the evening.

Our dads have to sit in a special row of men. They're going to carry the casket to the graveyard. We file past them without looking, and the music gets louder. The casket sits like an open suitcase up front. After we sit down in our wooden folding chairs all we can see is a nose and some glasses. That's our grandpa up there, he won't be hollering at us ever again for chewing on the collars of our dresses or for throwing hangers out the upstairs window. He won't be calling us giggleboxes anymore. He doesn't even know we're all sitting here, listening to the music and the whispers. He is in our hearts now, which makes us feel uncomfortable. Wendell and I were separated as a precautionary measure; I can just see the tips of her black shoes. They have bows on them and mine have buckles. She is swinging hers a little bit so I start to swing mine a little bit too. This is how you get into trouble, so I quit after a minute and so does she.

Pretty soon the music stops and my mother starts crying into her Kleenex. My aunt's chin turns into a walnut, and then she's crying too. Their dad is dead. Wendell puts her shoe on the back of the chair in front of her and slides it slowly down until it's resting on the floor again. I do the same thing. We're not being ornery, though. A lady starts singing a song and you can hear her breath. I can see only one inch of her face because she's standing in front of the dads. It's a song from Sunday school but she's singing it slower than we do and she's not making the hand motions. I do the hand motions myself, very small, barely moving, while she sings.

Wendell's mom leans over and tells me something. She wants me to sit on her lap. She has a nickname for me that nobody else calls me. She calls me Jody and everyone else calls me Jo. She's not crying anymore, and her arms are holding me on her lap, against her good blue dress. It's too tight in the armpits but you can't tell from looking. My mom's got Wendell.

After a while everyone starts crying, except Uncle Evan, my grandma's brother who always spits into a coffee cup and leaves it on the table for someone else to clean up. My aunt rests her chin on my head and rearranges her Kleenex so there's a dry spot. I sit very still while the preacher talks and the mothers cry, not moving an inch, even though my arms don't have anywhere to go. Wendell keeps moving around but I don't. Actually, I don't feel very good, my stomach hurts. I'm too big to sit on a lap, my legs are stiff, and now my heart has a grandpa in it.

The fairgrounds are huge and hot, an expanse of baking bodies and an empty stage. There are guys monkeying around on the lighting scaffold, high in the air. Mostly they're fat, stoned, and intent on their tasks, but Wendell's spied one that might be okay. Ponytailed and lean, he has his T-shirt off and stuck in the waistband of his jeans. I can't look at him because he's too high up, hanging off of things that don't look reliable. Wendell trains her binoculars on him, focuses, and then sets them down. "Yuck," she reports.

We will see God this afternoon — this is an Eric Clapton concert. We're sitting on one of our grandmother's worn quilts, spread out on the ground twenty feet from the stage. "Hey, look." I show Wendell a scrap of fabric. It's blue-and-red plaid with dark green lines running through. She and I used to have short-sleeved shirts with embroidered pockets made out of that material. On the ride over here we each took a small blue pill, a mild hallucinogen, and now Wendell has to put her face about an inch away from the quilt in order to get a sense of the scrap I'm talking about.

"It used to be seersucker," she says sadly. "And now it isn't." We think that over for a few minutes, how things change, how nothing can be counted on, and then Wendell remembers something. "My shirt had a pony on the pocket and yours had a *schnauzer.*" She snickers.

For some reason that irritates me no end. I hadn't thought of that schnauzer in years, and she has to bring it up today.

Thanks a whole hell of a lot. It did used to be seersucker, too, which is very strange, because now it's not. What could have happened to it? How can something go from being puckered to being unpuckered? You could see if it was the other way around, but this just doesn't make sense. My halter top keeps feeling like it's coming undone.

We put the cooler over the unsucked seersucker so we can quit thinking about it. Wendell stretches out on her back and stares at the sky. I stretch out on my stomach and stare at some grass. We are boiling hot but we don't know it, my hair is stuck to my back and Wendell's is standing straight up in a beautiful manner.

"Your hair is standing straight up in a beautiful manner," I tell her. She nods peacefully. She holds her arms up in the air and makes a *c* with each hand.

"I'm cupping clouds," she says. I try to pay closer attention to my grass, which is pretty short and worn down. It looks like it's been grazed. I read somewhere once that hysterical fans used to eat the grass where the Beatles had walked.

"Do you think Eric Clapton walked on this grass?" I ask Wendell. She looks over at me and considers. She thinks for so long that I forget the question and have to remember it again.

"No," she says finally. I feel relieved.

"Well then, I'm not eating it," I tell her flatly.

"Okay," she replies. I wish she had said "Okey-dokey" but she didn't. She said "Okay," which has an entirely different meaning.

I sit up and my halter top sags alarmingly. All I can do is hold it in place. There's nothing else to be done, I wouldn't have any idea how to retie it. Wendell is curled up in a ball next to me with her eyes shut.

"My top is falling off," I tell her. She doesn't open her eyes. I can feel sweat running down my back like ball bearings. Wendell groans.

"The clouds are cupping *me* now," she says. "Get them off." She's still got her eyes shut, making a whimpering sound. I don't know exactly what to do because I can't see any clouds on her and my shirt is falling off. I have to think for a moment. If I had just taken one bite of grass this wouldn't have happened.

A guy on the blanket next to us tries to hand me a joint. I can't take it because I'm holding my chest. He looks at me, looks at Wendell balled up on the ground, and nods knowingly. "Bummer," he proclaims.

I can't stand to have Eric Clapton see me like this. I let go of my shirt for one second and wave my arms over Wendell. My halter top miraculously stays in place. In fact, it suddenly feels too tight. "I just got the clouds off you," I inform her. She opens one eye, then the other, and sits up.

"You look cute," she tells me. She's turning pink from the afternoon sun and her hair is hectic and alive. We open beers from our cooler and start having fun.

By the time old Eric comes out, we've completely forgotten about him, so it's a pleasant surprise. We climb up on our cooler and dance around, waving our arms in the air. We're so close to the stage he is almost life-size. This is amazing. We dance and mouth the words while Eric sings tender love songs about George Harrison's wife and plays his guitar in a godlike manner.

The sky has turned navy blue. Eric stands in a spotlight on the stage. I pick him up once, like a pencil, and write my name in the air, then put him back down so he can play his guitar again. My halter top stays stationary while I dance around inside it naked. *Darling*, we sing to Eric, *you look won-der-ful tonight*. The air is full of the gyrations of six thousand people. My cousin is covered with clouds again but she doesn't seem to notice. Although it's still five months until Christmas, tiny lights wink on and off in her hair.

The tablecloth is covered with pie crumbs and empty coffee cups, a space has been cleared for the cribbage board and ashtrays. The sisters are smoking, staring at their cards, and talking about relatives. Neither of them can believe that Bernice is putting indoor-outdoor carpeting in her kitchen.

"You can't tell her a thing," my mother says. She lays down a card and moves her red peg ahead on the board.

"Shit," my aunt says softly. She stares at her cards. One of the husbands comes in for more pie. "What do I do here?" she asks him. He looks at her hand for a moment and then walks around the table to look at my mother's hand. He points to a card, which she removes and lays down. "Try that on for size," she tells my mother.

The back door flies open and two daughters enter. There is a hullabaloo. Barbie's little sister, Skipper, was sitting on the fence and accidentally fell off and got stepped on by a pig. "She's wrecked," Wendell reports. "We had to get her out with a stick." I show them the stick and Wendell shows them Skipper.

"Stay away from the pigs," my aunt says. She's looking at her cards.

"We *were* staying away from the pigs," I answer, holding up the muddy stick as evidence. "Tell them to stay away from *us*, why don't you?" My mother looks up. "Well," I say to her.

"You might find out *well*, if you're not careful," she tells me.

Wendell takes a whiff of Skipper, who is wearing what used to be a pair of pink flowered pajamas. A small bit of satin ribbon is still visible around her neck, but the rest, including her smiling face, is wet brown mud and something else. "Part of this is *poop*," Wendell hollers.

My aunt turns around finally. "Take that goddamn doll outside." She means business so we go upstairs, put Skipper in a shoe box, and find our Barbies.

"Mine's going to a pizza party," I say. My Barbie has a bubble haircut, red, and Wendell's has a black ponytail.

"Let's just say they're sitting home and then Ken comes over and makes them go to a nightclub," Wendell suggests. Hers doesn't have a pizza-party outfit so she never wants mine to get to wear one either.

"Mine's going to sing at the nightclub then," I warn her.

"Well, mine doesn't care," Wendell offers generously. She's eyeballing a white fur coat hanging prominently in my carrying case. Her Barbie walks over to mine. "Can I wear your fur tonight?" she asks in a falsetto.

"If I can wear your bola," my Barbie replies.

"It's boa, stupid," Wendell tells me. She digs out a pink feathered scrap, puts it in her Barbie's hand, and makes her Barbie throw it at mine.

"Let's say it's really hot out and they don't know Ken is coming over and they're just sitting around naked for a while," I suggest.

"Because they can't decide what to wear," Wendell clarifies. "All their clothes are in the dryer." She wads up all the outfits lying around and throws them under the bed.

"Oh God, it's so hot," my Barbie tells hers. "I'm going to sit at the kitchen table." Naked, she sits down in a cardboard chair at a cardboard table. Her hair is a smooth auburn circle, her eyes are covered with small black awnings, her legs are stuck straight out like broomsticks.

Black-haired, ponytailed Barbie stands on tiptoe at the cardboard sink. "I'm making us some pink squirrels," she announces. "But we better not get drunk, because Ken might come over."

Both Barbies do get drunk, and Ken does come over. He arrives in an ill-fitting suit, and the heat in the Barbie house is so overwhelming that he has to remove it almost immediately.

"Hey baby," Ken says to no one in particular. The Barbies sit motionless and naked in their cardboard kitchen, waiting for orders. This is where Dirty Barbies gets murky — we aren't sure what's supposed to happen next. Whatever happens, it's Ken's fault, that's all we know.

The Barbies get tired and go lie down on their canopied bed. Ken follows them in and leans at a forty-degree angle against their cardboard dresser. He's trying to tell them he's tired, too.

"You're going to prison, buddy," Wendell finally says, exasperated. She heaves him under her bed and we get our Barbies up and dress them.

"Ken better not try anything like *that* again," ponytailed Barbie says. She's wearing a blue brocade evening gown with the white fur coat, and one cracked high-heeled shoe.

"He thinks he's funny but he's not," my Barbie replies ominously. "He's in jail and *we're* the only ones who can bail him out." She's got on a yellow satin-and-net dress with a big rip up the back, and the boa is wrapped tightly around her neck. By the time they get Ken out of jail and into his tuxedo, the whole evening is shot. The judge has to be bribed with a giant nickel that ponytailed Barbie holds in her outstretched hand.

"Crap," Wendell says when they holler at us from downstairs. I pack up my carrying case, drag it down the steps and out to the car. I keep sitting down the whole way because I'm tired.

"Get moving," my mother tells me. My aunt calls me Jody and gives me a little whack on the behind, but she doesn't mean anything by it. I climb in beside my sister and roll down the window.

"Whaaa," Wendell says to me. This is the sound her Betsy-Wetsy makes when it gets swatted for peeing.

The car pulls out onto the highway and turns toward town.

I left my Barbie's pizza-party outfit under Wendell's pillow so she could use it until next time. Too bad, I miss it already. Red tights and a striped corduroy shirt with tassels that hang down. It goes better with a bubble cut than a ponytail, really. I should never have left it.

August, early evening. We're crammed into Uncle Fred's yellow Caddie, driven by Little Freddy, our cousin. I have on a low-backed, peach-colored dress with spaghetti straps and a giant, itching wrist corsage made of greenery and tipped carnations. Wendell is wearing an ivory wedding gown with a scoop neck and a hundred buttons down the back. It's the dress our grandmother married our grandfather in and it makes Wendell look like an angel. There are guys present — my boyfriend, a sweet, quiet type named Eric, and Wendell's brand-new husband, Mitch, a mild-mannered, blue-eyed farmer who is gazing at the cornfields streaking by.

Cousin Freddy is in control at this point, possibly a big mistake. One misplaced elbow and all the windows go down at once, causing hot air to whirl around inside the Caddie, stirring up everyone's hair and causing a commotion. "Okay, okay," Freddy says in a rattled voice. He pushes another button and all the windows go back up, the commotion stops, the air conditioning comes back into play.

Wendell has a wreath of baby's breath perched on top of her head like a crown of thorns. A slight crevice has appeared in the front of her hair, the baby's breath has lifted with the landscape and sits balanced on two distinct formations. The back is untouched. She wrestles herself over to the rearview mirror and gets a glimpse.

"Oh my God, it's the Red Sea," she says. "You parted my *hair*, Freddy."

There is an audible combing noise inside the car for a moment as she tries to impose some discipline on it. Freddy looks at her in the rearview mirror. He's got Uncle Fred's five-o'clock shadow and Aunt Velma's tiny teeth, he's wearing a powder blue short-sleeved shirt and a flowery necktie, fashionably wide. "We can borrow you a rake at one of these farmhouses," he says, braking. The Caddie, dumb and obedient as a Clydesdale, slows down, makes a left and then a right, pulls onto a dirt track leading into a cornfield. Freddy gets his wedding present from under the seat, lights it, and passes it back. We pile out into the evening and stand, smoking, next to the car.

The sky is way up there, a lavender dome. There's a gorgeous glow of radiation in the spot the sun just vacated, a pale peach burst of pollution that matches my dress. The corn is waxy and dark green and goes on forever. We're standing in a postcard.

"This is my big day," Wendell mentions. The crown of thorns is resting peacefully, swifts are swooping back and forth, drinking bugs out of the sky. We're trying to keep the hems of our dresses from dragging in the dirt.

"This corn is *ready*," Mitch says quietly, to no one in particular. The stalks are taller than us by a foot, a quiet crowd of ten million, all of them watching us get high and wreck our outfits.

"Don't lean on the car," I tell Wendell. She stands in her usual slouch, one arm wrapped around her own waist, the other bringing the joint to her lips. She squints and breathes in, breathes out. "You look like Lauren Bacall only with different hair," I say.

She considers that. "You look like Barbara Hershey only with a different face," she says kindly. We beam at one another. This is Wendell's big day.

"Hey, bats," Eric says suddenly. He's looking up into the air where the swifts are plunging around. I'm very fond of him for a moment, and then I feel a yawn coming on. A breeze has picked up and the corn is rustling, a low hiss from the crowd. We're making Wendell late to her own party.

The Caddie takes us out of the cornfield, haunch-first. Freddy steers it up to the highway, sets the cruise, and we all lean back, stare out the side windows, and watch the landscape go from corn to soybeans to cows to corn. Next thing you know we're getting out again, this time at Wendell's old house, the farm.

The wedding cake is a tiered affair with peach-colored roses and two very short people standing on top. Our mothers made the mints. This is a big outdoor reception, with a striped awning and a skinned pig. The awning is over a rented dance floor, the pig is over a bed of coals. There are as many relatives as you'd want to see in one place; the men standing around the revolving pig, the women putting serving spoons in bowls of baked beans, potato salad, things made with Jell-O, things made with whipped cream, things made with bacon bits.

Two uncles are tapping the beer keg. They keep drawing up tall glasses of foam and dumping it on the ground.

"I need a beer bad," Wendell says. She touches her head. "How's the crown?"

"Firm," I tell her. We get ourselves two glasses of foam to carry around and wander over to the food tables.

"This has prunes in it, if you can believe that," an aunt tells us, uncovering a bowl full of something pink that just came from the trunk of her car. Our mothers are standing at a long table where more women are unwrapping gifts and logging them in a book. Wendell's mother is wearing a long dress, gray silk with big peach-colored roses and green leaves down the front. My mother has on a pantsuit that everyone keeps admiring. They're both wearing corsages. "Ooh," my aunt says. A box has just been opened containing an enormous macramé plant hanger, with big red beads and two feet of thick fringe.

"Holy shit," Wendell says, taking a drink of foam.

The guests eat salads and chips and pig, the sky turns pewter, deep cobalt, then black. The band strikes up; four guys, two of them relatives. They play a fast number and everyone under the age of ten gets out there to dance. The littlest kids concentrate on trying to get it exactly right, swinging their hips and whirling their arms around. After about two songs all of them are out of control and sweating, hair stuck to their head, girls seeing who can slide the farthest on patent-leather shoes, boys taking aim and shooting each other with their index fingers without mercy. The parents have to step in, remove a few examples, and put them in chairs. One gets spanked first for calling his mother a dipshit in front of the whole crowd.

A waltz begins to play and the older couples move out onto the floor, husbands with wives, various uncles with various aunts. My own dad dances me around a few times, tells me my dress is pretty, and delivers me in front of Eric, who looks stupendously bored and not quite stoned enough. "Hey, lotta fun," he says insincerely. I make him go dance with my mom.

Wendell takes a break from talking to people and we pull up lawn chairs next to the dance floor. Her ivory dress shines in the darkness. "I keep losing my drink," she says. We share a full, warm beer that's sitting on the ground between our chairs, passing it back and forth, watching the fox-trotters.

"I wish I could do the fox-trot," I say wistfully.

She nods. "We can't do anything good," she says wearily.

"We can two-step," I answer, in our defense.

"Yeah," she says through a yawn. "But big whoop, the two-step." Two short great-aunts glide by at a smart clip and wave at us, the bride and the bridesmaid. Wendell waves back like a beauty queen on a float, I smile and twinkle my fingers. "Yee-haw," I say quietly. On the other side of the dance floor Mitch stands listening intently to one of our distant, female relatives.

He winks at us when she isn't looking and we wink back hugely. "That's my first husband, Mitch," Wendell says fondly.

The night air is damp and black against my arms, like mossy sleeves. There are stars by the millions up above our heads. Wendell and I are sitting directly under Gemini, my birth sign, the oddball twins, the split personality. Part of me wants to get up and dance, the other part wants to sit with my head tipped back. All of me wants to take off my wrist corsage.

"Nice ragweed corsage," I tell Wendell. My arm itches like fire, long red hives are marching up to my elbow. I take it off and put it under my chair.

"Give it a heave," she suggests, and I do. It lands within twenty feet of our lawn chairs. A giant calico farm cat steps out from nowhere, sniffs it, then picks it up delicately and fades back into the blackness. Under the awning the air is stained yellow, the band is playing a disco song. Our mothers are in the midst of a line dance, doing their own version of the Hustle, out of synch with everyone else. Their work is done, they've mingled, they've been fairly polite. Now they've got about twenty minutes of careening before they collapse in lawn chairs and ask people to wait on them. They're out there trying to kick and clap at the same time, without putting their drinks down. I decide I'd better join them.

My mother's cheeks are in bloom, from sloe gin and exertion, her lipstick has worn off but her corsage is still going strong, a flower the size of a punch bowl. She tries for the relaxed shuffle-kick-pause-clap of all the other line dancers but can't do it. She sets her drink down at the edge of the dance floor where it's sure to get knocked over and comes back to the line, full steam ahead. She starts doing the Bump with Wendell's mom and another aunt. Before they can get me involved, I dance myself over to the edge of the floor and step out into the darkness.

"The moms need to be spanked and put in chairs," I tell Eric, who hands over his beer without being asked. He looks peaceful and affectionate; his hair is sticking straight up in front and there's something pink and crusty all over the front of his shirt.

"One of those kids threw a piece of cake at me," he says placidly. He's been smoking pot out in the corn with Freddy, I can tell. The band pauses between numbers and the mothers keep dancing. In the distance, two uncles stand talking, using the blue glow of a bug zapper to compare their mangled thumbnails. Up by the band, the bride is getting ready to throw the bouquet. I'm being summoned to come stand in the group of girl cousins clustered around Wendell. I walk backward until I'm past the first row of corn, Eric following amiably, pink-eyed and slap-happy. He's using a swizzle stick for a toothpick.

Inside the corn it is completely dark, the stalks stand silent, the sounds of the party are indistinct. We can hear each other breathing. There is a muffled cheering as the bouquet gets thrown, and then someone talks loud and long into the microphone, offering a toast. Eric begins nuzzling my ear and talking baby talk.

"Hey," I whisper to him.

"Mmmm?" he says.

"Have you ever seen a corn snake?"

He refuses to be intimidated. A waltz begins and we absently take up the one-two-three, one-two-three. Around us the dark stalks ripple like water, the waves of the blue Danube wash over us. "I can show *you* a corn snake," he says softly, into my hair.

Here is a scene. Two sisters talk together in low voices, one knits and the other picks lints carefully off a blanket. Their eyes meet infrequently but the conversation is the same as always.

"He's too young to retire," my mother says. "He'll be stuck to her like a burr, and then that's all you'll hear. How she can't stand having him underfoot." One of my uncles wants to retire from selling Motorola televisions and spend the rest of his years doing woodworking.

"How many pig-shaped cutting boards does anybody need?" my aunt says. She holds her knitting up to the window. "God*damn* it. I did it again." She begins unraveling the last few rows, the yarn falling into a snarl around her feet.

"Here," my mother says, holding out a hand, "give me that." She takes the ball of pale yellow yarn and slowly, patiently winds the kinked part back up. While they work, a nurse enters and reads a chart, takes a needle from a cart in the hall, and injects it into the tube leading into my mother's arm. When the door snicks shut behind her, my aunt quits unraveling long enough to get a cigarette from her purse.

"They better not catch me doing this," she says, lighting up. She's using an old pop can for an ashtray. The cigarette trembles slightly in her long fingers and her eyes find the ceiling, then the floor, then the window. She adjusts the belt on her suit, a soft green knit tunic over pants, with silver buttons and a patterned scarf at the neck. She's sitting in an orange plastic chair.

My mother is wearing a dark blue negligee with a bedjacket and thick cotton socks. She takes a puff from my aunt's cigarette and exhales slowly, making professional smoke rings. "Now I'm corrupted," she says dryly.

"If any of them walked in right now, they'd have a fit," my aunt replies uneasily. She's worried about stern daughters, crabby nurses.

"Do I give a good goddamn?" my mother asks peacefully. She's staring at the ceiling. "I don't think I do." She's drifting now, floating upward, her shot is taking effect. She gets a glimpse of something and then loses it, like a fish swimming in and out of view in the darkness under water. She struggles to the surface. "I hope you get a girl," she says.

My aunt is knitting again, the long needles moving against each other, tying knots, casting off, creating small rosettes. Wendell is ready to have a baby any day now. "Well, she's carrying it low," my aunt answers skeptically. The room is dimming, she turns her chair more toward the window. There is a long pause, with only the needles and the tedious breath, the sterile landscape of cancer country.

"That doesn't mean anything," my mother finally replies. Her father bends over the bed to kiss her, as substantial as air; he's a ghost, they won't leave her alone. She moves slowly through the fluid and brings a thought to the surface. "We carried all of ours low, and look what we got." They swim through her lake, gray-eyed sisters, thin-legged and mouthy. They fight and hold hands, trade shoes and dresses, marry beautiful tall men, and have daughters together, two dark-eyed cousins, thin-legged and mouthy. A fish splashes, a silver arc against the blue sky, its scales like sequins. She startles awake.

"I hope you get a girl," she says again. This is all she can think to say. Her sister, in the dimness, sets down her work and comes to the bed. She bends over and pulls the blanket up, straightens it out. She can't think of what to say either. The face on the pillow is foreign to her suddenly, distant, and the weight of the long afternoon bends her in half. She leans forward wearily, and lets herself grimace.

"We got our girls we wanted so bad, didn't we?" my mother whispers to her, eyes still shut. My aunt straightens and fingers a silver button at her throat.

"Those damn brats," she comments. She presses both hands against the small of her back and shuts her eyes briefly. For an instant she sees the two original brats — wearing their droopy calico dresses, sassing their mother, carrying water up from the pump at the home place, knocking into each other. "You were always my sister," she says softly.

My mother is completely without pain now, the lake is dark, the fish move easily out of her way. Her sister swims by and makes a statement. "I know it," she answers. She tries to think of a way to express something. Sequins fall through the water, fish scales, and a baby floats past, turned upside-down with a thumb corked in its mouth. The morphine is a thin vapor in her veins. She rouses herself.

"He did do a nice job on those Christmas trees," she says. My aunt nods. She's talking about the woodworking uncle now, who made Christmas trees for all the sisters to put in the middle of their dining-room tables.

"I told him to make me a couple more for next year," my aunt says. "My card club went nuts over it." She lights another cigarette, hating herself for it. My mother is silent, her hands cut the water smoothly, like two long knives. The little gray-eyed girls paddle and laugh. She pushes a spray of water into her sister's face and her sister pushes one back. Their hair is shining against their heads.

In the dimness of the hospital room, my aunt smokes and thinks. She doesn't see their father next to the bed, or old Aunt Grace piddling around with the flower arrangements. She sees only the still form on the bed, the half-open mouth, the coppery wig. She yawns. Wendell's stomach is out to here, she remembers, any day now. That's one piece of good news.

My mother sleeps silently while my aunt thinks. As the invisible hands tend to her, she dives and comes up, breaks free of the water. A few feet over a fish leaps again, high in the air. Her arms move lazily back and forth, holding her up, and as she watches, the fish is transformed. High above the water, it rises like a silver baton, presses itself against the blue August sky, and refuses to drop back down.

Behind the Screen

I'*m looking at the backs of all their heads*. They're sitting on lawn chairs in the dusk and so am I, only their lawn chairs are on the lawn while mine is on the enclosed back porch. I have to look at the backs of their heads through the screen. We're waiting for the fireworks to begin.

My sister is wearing shorts, a midriff top, and all manner of jewelry — a pop-bead necklace, a Timex wristwatch, a mood ring, and a charm bracelet that makes a busy metallic rustle every time she moves her arm, which she does frequently. On the charm bracelet, between a high-stepping majorette and a sewing machine with movable parts, is a little silver book that opens like a locket to display The Teen Commandments. Engraved in infinitesimal letters: *Don't let your parents down, they brought you up; Choose a date who would make a good mate; and* the famous *At the first moment turn away from unclean thinking — at the first moment*. It has such an urgent tone it forces you to think uncleanly. Right now my sister is sitting in a lawn chair waiting for it to get dark. Every few minutes she raises and lowers her right arm so the charm bracelet, which I covet, clanks up to her elbow and then slides slowly and sensuously back down to her wrist. She doesn't bother turning around to see how I take this. She knows it's killing me.

They won't let me off the porch because I'm having an allergy attack. A low whistling sound emanates from my chest whenever I breathe. I can put a little or a lot of force behind it, depending on my mood. I'm allergic to ragweed and thistles and marigolds and dandelions and daisies, so we're all used to me being stuck on the porch while everyone else is having fun. Also grass; I'm allergic to grass. Right now one nostril is completely plugged up while the other runs in a steady drip.

My four-year-old brother is wearing cowboy boots and shorty pajamas, a gunbelt minus the guns, and a hat with earflaps. He's shooting each member of my family in turn with his crayon-size index fingers. He smiles at me, his little teeth glinting in the dusk. "You dead," he says.

I press my face up against the screen. It smells like dirt. I put my tongue out tentatively. It tastes like dirt. "Go to H," I say.

My mother turns her head halfway around and looks into my father's ear. "You're gonna get a whole lot sicker, miss," she tells me. Stars are beginning to be visible through the cloudy beehive of her teased hair. It's the Fourth of July 1962, and our city is having a fireworks display in the park. I have my own bowl of popcorn on the porch, and a glass of pop. The fireworks will be visible over the top of the dying elm tree in our backyard. It's impossible for me to eat the popcorn because I'm wearing a nose tourniquet, an invention I came up with myself: half of a twisted Kleenex, one end stuffed into one nostril, the other end in the other nostril. It has a wicking effect, and saves the effort of swabbing all the time.

"I can't even taste this pop," I say to the screen, after taking a sip. They all ignore me. The family dog, Yimmer, is sitting on my father's lap, growling quietly each time my brother shoots her.

My sister takes a loud swig out of a bottle of Pepsi, wipes her mouth elaborately, and says, "Man, was that good."

I examine a series of interesting scabs on my right knee. None of them are ready to be removed, although a couple are close. "You should see these scabs," I say to the backs of their heads.

My brother marches in place, talking to himself in a stern whisper.

My mother lights another Salem and positions a beanbag ashtray on the metal arm of her chair.

My father leans down and gives Yimmer's head a kiss.

Suddenly the scruffy edges of the elm tree are illuminated. The night sky turns pale above the garage, staccato gunfire, and a torpedo of light wiggles upward, stops, and fizzles. There is a beat of silence and then a burst of cascading pink and green worms. A long sigh is heard, from my family and the family next door.

I have my forehead against the screen, breathing in the night air and the heavy, funereal scent of roses, the only flower I'm not allergic to. A noodle skids across the sky, releasing a shower of blue spangles, jewels on a black velvet bodice. Way up there is outer space. I lean back and touch my forehead; an indented grid from the screen has been pressed into it. All these fireworks are somehow scaring me. "You should see my forehead," I say to my mother's hair.

"What's wrong with it?" she asks patiently. She doesn't turn around.

"I keep pressing it on the screen," I say.

"Don't push on that screen," my father says.

"I'm not," I say.

The sky is full of missiles. All different colors come out this time, falling in slow motion, red and blue turning to orange and green. It's so beautiful, I have to close my eyes. My family joins the neighbors in oohing. Suddenly, as the delayed booms are heard, I have to lean forward and put my head on my knees, inhaling the scent of Bactine and dirt. Everything is falling away from me. I open my eyes.

Black sky, dissipating puffs of gray smoke, the barely visible edges of the elm tree. My father's hand is dark against the white of the dog's fur. My brother is aiming both forefingers at the sky. A match flares suddenly; my mother touches it to her cigarette and inhales.

I am stuck somewhere between the Fourth of July and the rest of time, the usual chaos inside my head distilled down into nothing. I put my cheek against the screen, feeling the grid. There is an uproar, gunfire, sounds from the crowd.

Shooting stars in the cold of outer space; one after another the missiles are launched until the sky is brilliant with activity and smoke. Huge arcs of pink and yellow. Orange things that fizzle for an instant and then send out sonic booms. Long terrible waterfalls of yellow and blue. In the brightness, the backs of all their heads look rapt. My brother has his hands over his ears. My sister's mouth is open. The dog has her head in my father's armpit. It goes on for minutes, the booming sounds and the brilliant light. Closing my eyes doesn't work, it makes me feel like I'm falling backward. Instead I watch their hair, all the different styles right in my own back yard, and say The Teen Commandments quietly to myself: *Avoid following the crowd; be an engine, not a caboose. Stop and think before you drink.* Gunfire, one last wild spiraling of colors, and it's over.

"I'm not going to bed," my brother says resolutely.

The dog jumps down and stretches.

I remain in my lawn chair as they all troop into their house. One of my sister's better personalities comes out and she stops to comb her fingers through my hair and carries my full popcorn bowl into the house.

"She can't eat a thing," she tells my mother piously.

"Bath," my mother says to her. I hear my sister stomp up the stairs and then I hear my brother stomp up behind her, two feet on each stair.

"I saw a goddamned mosquito in here," my mother says. There's some flailing around, the whap of the flyswatter, and then my dad says, "Ick." The freezer opens, a bowl is clattered out of the cupboard. Ice cream. There's the unscrewing sound of a jar opening. Marshmallow stuff. My head hurts. I remove my spent nose tourniquet and start twisting a new one. Before I can get it in place there is a damp trickle on my lip.

"You guys?" I say. Any minute now they're going to send me upstairs.

There's an expectant pause in the kitchen.

"This lawn chair is stuck to my legs," I tell them.

A bottle is opened and an audible swig is taken. The lighter snaps and there's silence while she exhales.

Uh-oh.

"Bath," she says.

Coyotes

A small gesture of movement, a hiss of grass, and he is frozen stone for an instant, yellow eyes pinned on the spot, ears cocked forward. A quick lunge of muscles and paws, a darting switchback, and suddenly a rabbit is beating itself to death inside his mouth, against his tongue. This is lunch, unexpected.

In the tall papery weeds he pants and heaves and eventually, regretfully, begins licking the red off his paws. This will lead, as always, to the licking of his whole body, the coarse mangy fur like sawgrass against his tongue. He spreads the toes of one back paw and gnaws something hard and spiny away from the pad. He shakes his head fiercely to dislodge it from his teeth and then groans, rolls over flat on his side. He is in a trance now, one lobe of the brain completely at rest, in a smooth white fog that settles completely, like bedcovers, and doesn't lift until dark. The other lobe is on edge, senses opened so wide they collect amazing things: the screaming of unseeable insects hopping from one hair follicle to another; the droning currents emanating from power lines a quarter mile away; the throbbing of water deep beneath the ground. In the fog each paw twitches in preparation for the leap, the bite, the flat-out escaping run. Through the mist creeps a glowing, dull-witted bunny, eyes stupid, tail erect. Yellow paws pulse against the dirt as the coyote closes over its belly and suddenly the bunny is a chicken and the prized feel of it — white feathers beating softly against his muzzle — causes him, like a dog being petted, to wag heavily against the grass and bark lightly in sleeping pleasure.

In my dreams the ground murmurs over and over, until I'm ready to wake up swinging. *I am Kansas*, it says, *I am Kansas I am Kansas I am Kansas.* This is a train headed for Arizona and those are other passengers. The guy across from me has on house slippers and a hat because it's freezing in here. He's reading a book with a sprawled dead woman on the cover. Beside me, Eric is sleeping with his neck exposed and both hands lying open and empty. God. I put my own hands back into my armpits, bring my knees up, bend my head down, and try to sink back into some kind of blankness. Inside my mind a green and brown landscape appears, a mountain hillside with white-tailed deer arranged here and there, a stump, a path, a clump of rocks. Old slides from past vacations click into place and then disappear, one after another. The wheels drone. A burned forest, the sharp gaze of a fox, a pair of ponies standing at a fence, wildflowers, and broken barns; they each snap into position, linger while I look, and then make way for the next. Beneath me the gravelly ground goes on and on, explaining itself in dull tones: *I am Kansas I am Kansas I am Kansas.*

———

Small- to medium-size creatures creep and coil themselves over the desert floor, making their separate ways toward their separate destinies. Big creatures drive their cars along its roads and mostly don't get out, except to take leaks at the edge of the blacktop. Or point their cameras, hesitate, and give up. It looks different through the lens than through the windshield. Empty and blank and pointless.

I'm in a green tent that turned luminous a few minutes ago when the sun hit it. Eric is cooking breakfast and I'm lying in a sleeping bag not wanting to get up. It is freezing, that much is definitely true. And my shoulders hurt from too much sun and the ground is hard as a city street.

"Come on and get up," Eric calls. "It's warm out here." I peel up a corner of the green door and see him turning omelets with one gloved hand. The other is inside his coat pocket. He's got binoculars around his neck and a purple wool baseball cap on his head. He looks like a maniac.

I'm getting up.

He roams in the blistering sunlight. The sand beneath his paws feels like fire. Every two or three miles he finds a spot of shade and stretches out, squinting into the distance, panting fast and loud. A quick movement, an interruption in the blankness of the sand, and he rises and runs, ears cocked, feet springing off the sandy ground. Mice and snakes. It takes several to make a meal. If the head of the snake rises in the air, he backs off, whining and growling; if not, he pursues it, sometimes winning, sometimes not. In his dreams at night the long limber bodies of the serpents move unexpectedly at him. Awake, he bites the heels of the beasts in the pastures, on the long empty range, dodging the hooves, tasting the dirt and dung and

good description of a coyote

the coarse fringe of fur. The coyote hates horses and mules, the lowing cows, rich men and poor men. He likes mice and rats, the birds that burst forth in a glorious fan of wings, a squawk.

He roams in the blistering sunlight. His stomach gnaws and his eyes become more alert. The scent of water rises in his consciousness, he presses his nose upward and springs into his lilting trot. Around water is food. The desert gives way to the dappled green of sparse bushes, billowing grass. The coyote tilts his head sideways and uses the round dish of his upright ear to bring in any sounds along the bank. He drinks, listens again, and settles himself to wait. He scratches the area right where his heart beats. Small sounds come forward tentatively from the buzzing emptiness. The grass begins to sway as the breeze picks up. The sun is receding; it is long past dinnertime. The current carries small sticks and leaves, twirling, past his face as the coyote watches the bank, still as stone, waiting for a creature to come forth. From the cover of the wavering rushes, the rabbits press low against the ground, against the urge to run-run-run. The riverbank breathes quietly and patiently; the coyote pins his eyes on a moving reed, turns his ear, lifts his muzzle slightly. A chipmunk leaves the shelter of the grass to step forward. A cluster of oblong seeds on the moist bank has called to him and he must obey.

Inside its green skin a frog blinks, a rectangular insect with a tender belly is claimed by a sticky tongue. The chipmunk squeaks once, the coyote wags and growls as he chews, the dying sun pinkens the air.

We are under a giant balanced rock. There are trees here with bark like alligator hide. Suitcases with leaves. Their roots pop up out of the shallow soil like bent knees poking out of bath-

water. We have canteens, just like cowboys, but the water
tastes old and filthy after it's been sitting in there. My shoes are
covered with dust and a mile ago a small, thick rattlesnake
buzzed at us from the edge of the trail. From above, this place
appears as rugged badlands, big craggy pinnacles sticking up
like blunt bayonets. The snake made me jumpy as all get-out
but I've already filed the image of it away — recoiling on itself,
the head a pulled-back wedge, its pattern subtle, smudged and
blended like a charcoal drawing on the rock's surface — to be
remembered later when I'm back in my own habitat, standing
on a linoleum floor somewhere. What I really want to see is a
javelina, but of course I won't. They're piglike things with
tusks and they run in small herds, snorting and huffling over
the pine needles and fallen logs at the bottom of this place. This
is a bowl of mountains and greens with tender pieces of meat
roaming here and there.

My thighs are on fire, from the burn of the sun and the exertion. From the lip of the bowl, up top, it looked more treach-
erous and lively than it turned out to be. The cleared overlook
at the tip of the trail, Massai Point, is named for a Chiricahua
Apache man who stole a horse out from under the droopy mustache of a settler. The startled, righteous white man gathered
up some of his buddies and they stood at the point and
watched for the Apache to show the top of his head. Rifles
poised and scanning, they kept their eyes peeled. From the
overlook there are a hundred thousand gaps and crevices between the balanced monoliths and stacked boulders. Breathing
into the granite walls, hands flat and calming against the heaving sides of his new horse, he waited them out, watching the
sky darken and the moon lift its face. They got tired of waiting
and rode back to their settlement, miffed at the giant shelter-
ing landscape, the defiant stone thumbs that hid wild Indians
in their shadows.

This is daytime. My soap opera is on right now, somewhere. Back in Iowa. My people are roaming back and forth on the television screen, all prepared for any kind of upheaval; there are a lot of chiffon dresses and dyed-to-match shoes. I mention to Eric that my show is on. He turns with a grin and watches me ski down a dissolving patch of trail. Loose rocks roll beneath my feet as I'm carried along. This is elementary physics, ancient Egyptians used it to take house-size rocks here and there, up and down various hills. I skid one foot halfway under an overhanging rock and a curled ribbon of skin peels up my leg. Rattlers hang out under rocks, waiting for a shin to come along. Yee-ikes. I pull my lower leg back out where it belongs and start making an enormous deal out of my injury. Eric sprinkles water on it and yawns. He remembers that we're an hour off down here, the soap is already over.

The air turns tangy and alive, the sun is gone, the sky is black. Glimmers of light bristle forward in the dome above the coyote's head. He moves out. The night has a seething quality, a crisp silence that hides the tunneling of small, cowering mammals, the slumped somnolence of the wandering cattle, the wide-eyed jitters of the stick-leg deer. The moon, from the bitter cold of outer space, croons to the griddle of the desert. The coyote listens and turns to the west. An image has moved forward in his head: Out of the murk a picture comes to the forefront, melting into view. The thick, spongy edges of lightness, the dark legs and face, the palpable panic of the herd. The sheep are waiting. The moon pushes him forward from behind and snakes slide under bushes until he passes. Out of nowhere a skunk appears, startled, hunkering low with wide mirrored eyes. The coyote darts, bites, and opens the belly with one efficient fang. He drags it around in a gleeful circle, then thrusts one shoulder at a time into the cooling wetness. It is night and feelings are rising up, like blood to a scrape.

The desert is lunar. Every so often a night bird courses low over the sand and the mice shudder, the lizards peer lidlessly around, unroll their tongues and reel them in again. The moon lowers itself, sitting for a few moments on the shoulders of a western butte, considering the lake of shadows. In its distant, porous memory, the moon can conjure up how it pulled the ice back like a bedsheet, exposing the tender ground beneath. The face on the butte is ice blue and furious, slumping beneath its shoulders infinitesimally, down and down, until it is gone and the stars are livid and blinking. The insects teem, the rodents scrabble, the night-blooming flowers push themselves open and await their guests.

We have two things going for us: a spectacular white rental car and a bag of red-hot cinnamon Fireranchers. We discuss for a fair amount of time while sucking on the Fireranchers whether it is right to "beat" a rental car more than you would beat your own car. We decide it isn't right, although we immediately follow that up by seeing how fast it can go on a stretch of gummy blacktop. It goes to one hundred and thirty miles an hour before it starts shivering.

The rental car has air conditioning but we're not using it. Instead we're keeping a spray bottle full of water in the cooler and spritzing ourselves with it every few miles. Now there is a contest to see who can put a new Firerancher in his or her mouth and not bite it for however long it takes it to disintegrate. I will lose this game and we both know it. We're playing it because we're stupendously bored but still in high spirits.

Every so often I put my foot on the dashboard for a leg inspection. My shinbone is a gentle, peeled blue. This is from when I fell down the mountain into the den of rattlesnakes.

"It wasn't a mountain, it was a path," Eric says. "And there weren't any rattlesnakes."

I spray cold water on my shin and then put my leg back down where it belongs. My whole body feels swampy. The air is a blast furnace and the windshield is a magnifying glass trained on our forearms. We are one moment from ignition. I turn the water bottle around and squirt myself flat in the face and then offer to do Eric.

"I'll do myself," he says threateningly. I hand the bottle over. It's not my style to squirt him with ice water while he's driving but predictably he falls apart for an instant and turns the bottle on me. It dries in one second from the hot breath coming through the window. We roll along in silence for awhile, sweating and thinking, working on our Fireranchers. Mine is so thin I try just resting my teeth on it to see how it feels. I bite it in half.

We are taking the low road from Tucson to a national monument on the border of Mexico. The map says we are now passing through the Comobabi Mountains, but outside the windows of our car the desert is as flat as a sheet of parchment. The saguaros have given way to brush and patches of gravelly dirt; along the highway from time to time are homemade altars. We keep passing them, eighty miles an hour. The next one we'll stop at so I can see who it's an altar to. There aren't even any jet trails out here, the sky is a long, blue yawn. Neil Young comes on the radio.

We see a hawk up ahead, standing on the hood of a broken-down car. We slow down to gaze and it stares at us. Its black-trousered legs are sturdy and long, its beak is curved. We peel off, back up to warp speed, and the landscape turns into a melting blur out the windshield.

"Look, sweetie," Eric says, turned toward me in the driver's seat.

On the very tip of his tongue is his Firerancher. Thin as tissue paper, it looks like the moon in the daytime sky. Suddenly love is looming over the car, as big and invisible as the ghost mountains of the Comobabi range. I smile at him and turn up the radio with my toes.

Connection?

He snaps peevishly at his haunch, bending stiffly backward to chew the peppery trail of a flea. The walls of the den are pungent with the smell of safety and his own fur. He gives up and flops back over, closes his eyes in the dimness and begins panting. No good, he's awake now, it's time to step back out into the day. In the sunlight he blinks and stretches, fore and aft, like a collie. He shakes so hard he almost knocks himself off his feet. The sky is as blue as blue and the coyote is in a good mood.

He lifts his muzzle and takes in a long snort of air, pulling with it the invisible happenings in the vicinity. There's something big and dead looming just over the rise. The coyote yawns and his tail swings down between his back legs in its traveling position. He puts his nose to the ground and begins his afternoon expedition. Somewhere, right on the edge of what his nose is capable of, a rabbity perfume is lingering. He breaks into a lope just for the fun of it but drops back down to a trot after a hundred yards or so. The sun is pressing burning fingers into his spine. The blacktop dips into view, and as the coyote moves toward it he prepares himself for the highway's big medicine. The sandy dirt beneath his paws gives way just a bit as each foot lands and springs off, the small stones and irregularities in his path add juice to his travels but rarely pain. Under his paws it is *sand . . . sand . . . rock . . . sand . . . stick . . . sand . . . stick* and then the highway's medicine: *hard . . .*

scalding . . . scalding . . . scalding and then *gravel . . . sand . . . rock . . . sand . . . sand . . . rock . . . sand* again.

As he passes once more safely through the hard pond of highway fire the coyote is startled by something in the air, something dangerous bearing down on him. Alert and agile, he jumps to the side, cringing and whining, but it is too late. An empty bread wrapper hits him smack in the side of the head.

The landscape has changed from the invisible Comobabi Mountains of love to the barren flats of boredom and annoyance. The sun is a yellow baseball hanging over right field, the driver's side is in the shade and the passenger's side is sizzling. I decide it's my turn to drive.

Eric glances over. "Uh, doubt it," he says.

I've just noticed how his hairline has taken a daring swoop down his forehead and back up again, just like his father's. I mention this to him while inspecting my fingernails.

He smiles and addresses me by my mother's name. "I mean, honey," he corrects himself, "the kid's got the wheel and the kid's keeping it." He's leaning back in his seat, steering with one finger, brow arched. We are very bored.

The kid is a shithook, I remark.

A shithook with the *wheel*, though, he clarifies. He points out that I'm sweating a lot, more than he's ever seen me do. "Pretty hot over there, eh?"

I begin calling him Lovey, and suggest that we change drivers without stopping. He gives in reluctantly, only because he knows eventually he'll lose. If I don't get to drive pretty soon I will open my car door while we're moving and he can't stand that. He's afraid I'll get sucked out by accident and it'll be his fault for being a control freak.

You have to be going really fast for this trick, over seventy miles an hour. Both of us recline our seats all the way down, I do the gas pedal with my left foot and hold the steering wheel steady with my left hand while Eric climbs into the back seat. I move over the gear shift and slide into his seat while he climbs over my reclined seat back into the passenger side. It's not exactly that smooth, of course, there is a lot of swerving and hollering that goes along with it. We settle in and bring our seat backs into position and open a can of malt liquor.

"Yee-haw," I say, now that I'm in the driver's seat. Eric tries to rig up a shade for his window using a white T-shirt. He can't get it to stay draped over while he rolls up the glass. I enjoy watching him do this a few times and then look sympathetic when he gives up. "Pretty hot over there, isn't it?" I ask him.

"Not really," he answers.

Twenty miles later we enter the Valley of the Ajo and head for the monument, right above the border of Mexico. The road is endless, with wavering lines of heat rising up and a mirage that looks like a silver pool always about half a mile ahead of the car. Suddenly Eric points and I press on the brake. Along the edge of the blacktop on the opposite side of the highway is a coyote, pushing a bread wrapper along with his nose. He ignores us completely, stops and puts one paw on the plastic wrapper, takes it in his teeth, and begins pulling it apart. He shakes his head like a dog. I pull off into the gravel and try to sit quietly, like I'm not a human. He's staring at me now, still nosing into the bag, gold eyes looking up from the dirty plastic.

The car is a boiling caldron. The coyote stands scruffy and skittish, like a wild dingo dog I met once, who bit everything in sight, wagging his tail like a maniac. Eric slides the camera to me and puts a hand on my arm. He whispers in my ear. I nod. I love dogs better than anything else on earth, next to cigarettes and a couple of people.

I find him in the lens, framed in a square. As I click the shutter he jumps sideways and takes off, running a few yards and then skidding to a halt, looking back over his shoulder. He's not afraid of us, he's just horsing around. In the rearview mirror he canters over the rocks, low to the ground, tail tucked. In the slide, projected on my living room wall, he will be a gray, moving blur, a running pelt. The gracious arms of an organ pipe cactus direct him up the hill, over the rise, out of the frame, and into memory.

The saguaros send out long lavender fingers into the afternoon. Grains of sand cool and then warm again as the slow sweep of the shadows moves past. Something looped and coiled unravels gradually, in no hurry, to follow the pool of purple, the spot where the shadow meets its source. It feeds a tongue out, testing the temperature of the air, and begins to wind back into the debris of the cactus again, until there is only a barely visible presence on the ground, a tangled rope with scales and eyes.

Nearly fifty feet in the air a scar, made with a pocketknife and dirty fingers, is visible on the skin of the cactus. A flicker lands on the green pinnacle and peers around, pokes the needle of its beak into the flesh, and peers again. A ridge ten miles west stands fluted and browning, like the crust of a pie, a hawk slides down a current of air and floats above it. The flicker thrusts again and shrugs the moisture down its throat.

The cactus receives the bird, tiny claws like pins, with the same indifference as it had the man with the pocketknife on the shuddering horse. Weak and boiling, he dug and dug into the spiny hide with his pocketknife. The horse died within the reach of the saguaro's shadow, descending into a dull bag that collapsed on itself, bones moving out across the desert floor in the mouths of jackals.

The man either made it or didn't. The words he spoke and the voice he spoke them in linger high above the ground nearly two hundred years later, buffeted by the hot wind, nourished by desperation and the terrible solitude. The flicker turns his head into the wind, finds the moisture again, drinks, and lifts off. The currents of air move around the top of the cactus, over the thorny scar.

Now, as then, the saguaro stands beneath the sun as the desert clock sweeps over the ground in circles, and begins the slow, tedious task of sealing its wound.

This is the campground: acres and acres of barren plots, bent and scraggy trees, stand-up grills, picnic tables, no people. One big vehicle is parked about a hundred yards away, on the other side of the bathrooms, tethered to an electrical hookup. The people won't come outside until the sun leaves, but a small apricot poodle ventures out a few times and barks at itself wildly. The door opens to let it back in, sending out a big waft of refrigerated air for the bugs and birds to enjoy.

Our tent is all set up, with a minimum of arguing. We stretch out inside it to see how long we can stand to lie there. First it gets very stuffy, then the air leaves completely. We climb out and sit in the front seat of the car, listening to the radio and eating potato chips, waiting for the sun to back off. I'm reading a book about vampires that is so graphic in various parts that I have to breathe through my mouth and stop eating chips. Eric is thumbing through an astronomy magazine. Every once in a while I'll tell him a detail from the vampire book and he'll show me his magazine, explain something about one of the pictures, a black background with white dots. We read and thumb until the landscape is a hazy 3-D postcard and the sky is a turquoise tent. Our legs decide to walk.

The Official Map and Guide stresses not once but twice that rattlesnakes are protected here. It has a curt, no-nonsense tone that indicates we'd better act right. Small quail run across the path, back and forth, stopping and starting, murmuring and pecking. In the distance one cactus stands apart, reaching at least two feet taller than any of the others, a surly foreman, the dad of the landscape. I want to go see it, see how tall it is compared to me.

Eric has a forked stick that he's using for a divining rod. "It'll come in handy for snakes," he tells me, "*and* show us where there's water." The stick suddenly lifts in the air and starts shaking, he manages to hold on and push it back down. "I accidentally pointed it towards the bathrooms," he says.

The camper people are out with their little dog. The guy has a garden hose that he's spraying the path with because he doesn't want dust from cars to get on his Astroturf rug. I feel like talking to him but he just nods without smiling and we have to keep walking. He points the hose politely in another direction until we're past, and the poodle barks and barks.

I tell Eric I wish I had a little dog like that one.

"Of course you do," he answers, "that's the one thing you're short on." Three dogs mingle and mill somewhere in the vast universe, in Iowa, wondering why we're not there petting them. I muse on this for a while. A big dog, a medium-size dog, and a charming lapdog with a mean streak.

"They don't even know we're gone," I tell Eric, "they think we went in the other room and just haven't come back yet." The minds of dogs interest me, the way they never bother to anticipate problems.

By the time we get to the tall cactus the light has softened to a benign burn, a warm pat on the head. We both look great all of a sudden, stained brown with pink auras. Eric sets down his stick and moves back to get the whole cactus in the frame, with me standing at the base for comparison. At the very top of the saguaro a crista has formed over some kind of damage. The scar blooms out, hard and dark green, like the tiny head on a giant. I step over the debris at the base and arrange myself with arms out, bent at the elbow. The cactus is very old and very tall; up close it is hard and weathered and looks important; a cactus emeritus.

I stand in the soft, end-of-day shadow and have my picture taken. It feels like being on Mars here, the light is strange, these green men stand all over the terrain.

Ninety-three million miles due west, the sun continues to shoot off its bottle rockets. The desert has edged away now, out of range. At the foot of the saguaro, a snake, without moving anything but the thread of tongue, gently touches shoe leather, considers it, and decides no. *Sounds like poetry*

The nervous birds are gone from the ground now, it is night. The coyote runs in a mile-wide circle, at a lope, thirty miles an hour. There is nothing else moving. The moon bounces in the sky, over his right shoulder, now behind. A rock rises, a cholla extends soft elbows in his path, a dry husk stares up from the ground. There is nothing. The moon is a wide, mottled face, the countenance of an enraged idiot. The coyote runs and runs, not gasping, until there is something.

Three mule deer spring and run in various directions, bounding, flinging their hooves in the air. He picks one and chases halfheartedly for a distance, hearing his own feet, feeling the moon. They reassemble farther out, staring at him through the dimness, long ears moving back and forth like wings, each face small and wary. The one he chased turns first and takes up its occupation again: finding forage and trying not to die. He holds the moment until he can stay still no longer and begins running again, away from the sky. The ground is silver, the rocks are gleaming. There is nothing.

We play euchre and hearts, drink beer, rearrange the lantern thirty times. Finally we put it under the picnic table and it i.-luminates our legs and shorts, blows the whistle on a iaぅge furred spider.

"It's got knees," I marvel. Actually, it has sort of a face, too, attached to a slender neck. I decide to sit on top of the table for a while.

"Let me get my spider stick," Eric says. He holds the tines of the divining rod and gently points the way for the spider. It scuttles a few feet and then pauses, goes back into a trance. "Get along, buddy," he urges, giving it a prod. It does several push-ups, puts a leg in the air, and then moves of its own volition out from under the table and into the darkness.

We play a few more hands of hearts, until I realize that we both want me to win and I still can't manage it. The whole desert is disappointed. We fold our hands and practice being bored for a while. Our dogs are sleeping at home, two of them nose to nose and snoring, one off by herself, flat on her side, dreaming of me. The stars are no match for the wash of the moon, the night air is navy blue and coolish against our skin.

The camper people are out of it. Their colored lanterns are dark now and the TV is on inside, the glow of Letterman and his guests reflected in the window. I can see a head framed in the light, surrounded by a frizz of hair. It's the poodle, looking at stars.

We clear the table and spread out a sleeping bag on it, flannel side up. This is the best way to watch the sky. Eric has his red flashlight and charts, I have my sweatshirt zipped and a Walkman with two pairs of headphones. It's his turn to choose a tape so I'm waiting for something discordant and spooky but when he pushes the button it's one of my favorites. *Thank you,* I mouth to him. He smiles, closes his eyes, and takes my hand. Side by side. He moves into the solitude of headphones and constellations. I am perched on planet Earth, Milky Way galaxy, who knows what universe. Way up there, satellites are parked with their motors running, and vivid rings of plasma do laps around Saturn. Way down here, there is only the terrible arch of the sky, the sagging moon, and nothing else.

The earphones make my head feel like a hollow tube, full of horns and drums and a voice that echoes like green glass. I am alone inside my own skin and the edges of everything have begun to darken slightly, curling and browning, the beginnings of disintegration. Inside my chest a heart begins knocking to get out. I am alone down here, and up there, clinging to the spoke of a satellite, looking upward at the dark velvet, and downward at the dark velvet.

There is nothing.

Pockmarked and surly, the moon steps back and drops the curtain, darkens the theater for the stars. The clock is halted, the desert gives up its heat. A finger-size lizard with infrared spots and oval eyes finds itself, one second too late, in the damp cotton of a mouth. Power lines gleam and bounce their signals on the ground, startling the brain waves of small mammals, putting thoughts in their heads. Something swims through the medium of sand and surfaces, pinches hard and holds on.

In the endless black of deep space a small comet hurtles along, tossing iceballs and dirt behind it, on a perpetual path, around and around and around, pointless and energetic. Propelled by the force of its combustion, the comet passes within

poem

poem

a light year of Sirius, burning out of control. Under the press of gravity and air, inside the earth's atmosphere, the coyote reads the signals in the ground, whirls, stops, and sprays a bush. He begins loping again, without awareness, the desire widening, a dark basin, until he cries as he runs, low and controlled. They are somewhere.

The moon is gone and Eric has fallen asleep beside me. Planets and stars. I know only the ones that everyone knows: the sun, the moon, the dippers, Gemini and Cancer. They move into formation, still and distant as dead relatives, outlining the shape of my mother's mouth. Nothing moves. Inside my head images emerge and retreat, emerge and retreat. I have to open my eyes. In the vivid blackness overhead a diamond falls through the sky, trailing its image, a split-instant of activity. By the time I realize I've seen it, the sky has recovered. I can't breathe in this emptiness. I turn on my side on the hard picnic table and look at Eric.

He is awake, watching me. He knows the desert is making me sad, that I have these moments; he smiles and moves up close. I can feel the sky on my face, the warm flannel of the desert floor below. I can feel the face of the man beside me. In the silence of the monument he begins whispering the names of the constellations while I listen: Cygnus the Swan, Pegasus the Horse, Canis Major the Great Dog, Cassiopeia, Arcturus.

I am on planet Earth.

Coyote

They are near. He pulls in the scent with loud snorts, running from bush to rock to bush again. This is a clearing, a high naked spot. On the distant rise, just ahead, waiting, they are still invisible, but the scent rises in the air around him, palpable as mist. He opens his mouth wide and stands frozen, ears back, eyes pressed shut. The dirt beneath his pads is hard and dry, devoid, the moon is gone.

As the mist rises around him, the sound comes forth, pulled from tendon and muscle. It pushes itself through his lungs and into the night, a long trembling wail, dying slowly, drifting finally, without his help, dissipating. Still frozen, he listens for a moment to the roaring silence, waiting, and slowly the sound moves back toward him, fainter, broken into parts like music. Many voices.

They are ahead of him, in the high clearing where the deer sometimes sleep, pausing to listen, ready to bring him in with the radar of their voices. He begins running again and gravity relinquishes its hold. The terrain becomes buoyant and he soars low over the ground, like a night bird, a skipped stone.

The tent is completely dark. I am floating on the ocean in a canoe, each dip of the oar pours out a panful of light, beneath the surface small silver minnows hover like aircraft. My big collie roams along the shore, following the boat, whining low in her throat, stamping her white paws against the sand. I row toward the beach, casting light behind me, and she begins to bark.

I am awake suddenly in the darkness. Outside the tent is the padding of feet, around and around, a swift turning, a pause. There is something in our campsite, trying to get our food. Eric startles and wakes, I touch his hair, breathe into his ear. The paws turn again, there is loud panting, the low whine, and then a series of barks and yelps, a prolonged terrible howl. It is deafening and wild, I can feel him out there, conjuring hysteria out of the dark. A long, plaintive keening, and suddenly it ends, drifting off, carried away from us. We are breathing low and shallow, resting on our elbows.

When the reply comes he joins in, barking first and then crying, pitched high then low, the howl of loneliness and communion. It is lunar and eerie, the pleading of the cold, dead moon to the blue and green revolving earth, the call of sister stars across years of space, the cry of a child who has lost her mother. Now it is coming from every side, the beautiful wailing; they are swarming over us, gray and brown ghosts, distant relatives.

In our green cocoon, we move closer to each other, hands, faces, knees. The walls of the tent press down like skin, the ground presses up like bone. The coyote is gone, suddenly, the air thins out and becomes ours again. Inside the narrow landscape of the tent, hills and valleys realign, adjust themselves, realign again with whispers.

The coyote runs, straining to reach the others, a quarter mile away, over the crest of the ridge. They are waiting for him in the darkness, in the burning desert with its lifted arms of cactus. In the dark tent, on my smooth ocean, inside my mind, he is there already, gray and golden like the desert, like the moon, moving among them in the clearing, feeling the thrust of snouts, the padding of many paws, the push of love.

Against the Grain

*I*t's okay to be married to a perfectionist, at least for a while. Just don't try to remodel a house with one, is all I can say. This is what he'll do: set you up with practice boards and nails to make sure you have the technique completely down before you attend to the task at hand, which he has suggested would be the best task for you at this particular time in your training. You sigh and jokingly threaten him with the hammer but because you aren't adept at pulling nails from ceiling trim you grudgingly work on the practice boards until you can almost remove a nail without splitting the wood all to hell. It makes your knees hurt to crouch that way so you take a doughnut break, staring out the dirty window at the neighbor's house across the way. The perfectionist comes in on his way from a completed task to a waiting, un-begun one. He notices you standing there and grins.

"It doesn't get done that way, does it?" he kids you.

You feel revitalized from the jelly filling and pour a tepid cup of coffee from the thermos, head back in, crouch some more. The pieces of trim are in pretty good shape, long stately things that will nestle up against the ceiling, hopefully hiding the uneven line between wallpaper and paint. The perfectionist is feeling very sensitive about that particular uneven line, since he tried and tried to make it straight. You assured him over lunch the previous day and again over dinner that the line would be covered up by the lovely trim. You, in fact, feel encouraged knowing that an uneven, almost jaggedy, edge will be hiding in the house. You tell the perfectionist this in a joking way and he stares at you for a long moment and then smiles uncertainly.

In the other room you can hear him giving explicit directions to his brother-in-law, who owes you guys a big favor for helping him put an oak floor in his den last summer. The perfectionist convinced him to go ahead and sand and refinish all the floors in the house while he was at it. After all, he explained, you might as well do it right. Then it's done and you can feel good about it. You know? His own sister didn't speak to the perfectionist for about three weeks after that, until the job was done and her furniture was back in place. He kept advising her to try another way whenever she got frustrated and started sanding wildly against the grain. Unfortunately, she knew that "try another way" is what they used to say to the retarded citizens at the sheltered workshop where he worked after college.

"I'm not retarded, pal," she told him.

No matter how hard you try, the long, lovely pieces of trim start out fine and end up with these odd-looking splits and splinters. He's whistling in the other room. You try a different technique than he showed you and suddenly the longest piece has become divorced from itself. Oh dear.

"Well," says the perfectionist, standing in the doorway. "We're having trouble, I see." He sets down his chisel and shows you once again how to tease the nail from the wood. "You can't just go nuts on it," he explains. "You can't *wrestle* it."

Carefully and efficiently, he sets himself to the task. Within fifteen minutes the wood is free of the nails, which are stacked, mostly unbent and ready to be used again, on a windowsill. You open the can of spackle with a screwdriver and begin the tedious job of filling all the little holes left behind. He's behind you before you know it.

His hair is tufted up in back from the hat he's been wearing and his pants have plaster dust on the knees. He has the sweetest face of any man you've ever seen. He smiles. "Just be sure not to glob it on," he says gently, and then retreats again, into the rest of the house, which is structurally unsound but possibly fixable, just like you.

The Fourth State of Matter

*T**he collie wakes me up about* three times a night, summoning me from a great distance as I row my boat through a dim, complicated dream. She's on the shoreline, barking. Wake up. She's staring at me with her head slightly tipped to the side, long nose, gazing eyes, toenails clenched to get a purchase on the wood floor. We used to call her the face of love.

She totters on her broomstick legs into the hallway and over the doorsill into the kitchen, makes a sharp left at the refrigerator — careful, almost went down — then a straightaway to the door. I sleep on my feet, in the cold of the doorway, waiting. Here she comes. Lift her down the two steps. She pees and then stands, Lassie in a ratty coat, gazing out at the yard.

In the porchlight the trees shiver, the squirrels turn over in their sleep. The Milky Way is a long smear on the sky, like something erased on a chalkboard. Over the neighbor's house,

Mars flashes white, then red, then white again. Jupiter is hidden among the anonymous blinks and glitterings. It has a moon with sulfur-spewing volcanoes and a beautiful name: Io. I learned it at work, from the group of men who surround me there. Space physicists, guys who spend days on end with their heads poked through the fabric of the sky, listening to the sounds of the universe. Guys whose own lives are ticking like alarm clocks getting ready to go off, although none of us is aware of it yet.

The collie turns and looks, waits to be carried up the two steps. Inside the house, she drops like a shoe onto her blanket, a thud, an adjustment. I've climbed back under my covers already but her leg's stuck underneath her, we can't get comfortable. I fix the leg, she rolls over and sleeps. Two hours later I wake up again and she's gazing at me in the darkness. The face of love. She wants to go out again. I give her a boost, balance her on her legs. Right on time: 3:40 A.M.

There are squirrels living in the spare bedroom upstairs. Three dogs also live in this house, but they were invited. I keep the door of the spare bedroom shut at all times, because of the squirrels and because that's where the vanished husband's belongings are stored. Two of the dogs — the smart little brown mutt and the Labrador — spend hours sitting patiently outside the door, waiting for it to be opened so they can dismantle the squirrels. The collie can no longer make it up the stairs, so she lies at the bottom and snores or stares in an interested manner at the furniture around her.

I can take almost anything at this point. For instance, that my vanished husband is neither here nor there; he's reduced himself to a troubled voice on the telephone three or four times a day.

Or that the dog at the bottom of the stairs keeps having mild strokes which cause her to tilt her head inquisitively and also to fall over. She drinks prodigious amounts of water and pees great volumes onto the folded blankets where she sleeps. Each time this happens I stand her up, dry her off, put fresh blankets underneath her, carry the peed-on blankets down to the basement, stuff them into the washer and then into the dryer. By the time I bring them back upstairs they are needed again. The first few times this happened I found the dog trying to stand up, gazing with frantic concern at her own rear. I praised her and patted her head and gave her treats until she settled down. Now I know whenever it happens because I hear her tail thumping against the floor in anticipation of reward. In retraining her I've somehow retrained myself, bustling cheerfully down to the basement, arms drenched in urine, the task of doing load after load of laundry strangely satisfying. She is Pavlov and I am her dog.

I'm fine about the vanished husband's boxes stored in the spare bedroom. For now the boxes and the phone calls persuade me that things could turn around at any moment. The boxes are filled with thirteen years of his pack-rattedness: statistics textbooks that still harbor an air of desperation, smarmy suitcoats from the Goodwill, various old Halloween masks and one giant black papier-mâché thing that was supposed to be Elvis's hair but didn't turn out. A collection of ancient Rolling Stones T-shirts. You know he's turning over a new leaf when he leaves the Rolling Stones behind.

What I can't take are the squirrels. They come alive at night, throwing terrible parties in the spare bedroom, making thumps and crashes. Occasionally a high-pitched squeal is heard amid bumps and the sound of scrabbling toenails. I've taken to sleeping downstairs, on the blue vinyl dog couch, the sheets slipping off, my skin stuck to the cushions. This is an affront to two of the dogs, who know the couch belongs to them;

as soon as I settle in they creep up and find their places between my knees and elbows.

I'm on the couch because the dog on the blanket gets worried at night. During the day she sleeps the catnappy sleep of the elderly, but when it gets dark her eyes open and she is agitated, trying to stand whenever I leave the room, settling down only when I'm next to her. We are in this together, the dying game, and I read for hours in the evening, one foot on her back, getting up only to open a new can of beer or take peed-on blankets to the basement. At some point I stretch out on the vinyl couch and close my eyes, one hand hanging down, touching her side. By morning the dog-arm has become a nerveless club that doesn't come around until noon. My friends think I'm nuts.

One night, for hours, the dog won't lie down, stands braced on her rickety legs in the middle of the living room, looking at me and slowly wagging her tail. Each time I get her situated on her blankets and try to stretch out on the couch she stands up, looks at me, wags her tail. I call my office pal, Mary, and wake her up. *"I'm weary,"* I say, in italics.

Mary listens, sympathetic, on the other end. "Oh my God," she finally says, *"what* are you going to do?"

I calm down immediately. "Exactly what I'm doing," I tell her. The dog finally parks herself with a thump on the stack of damp blankets. She sets her nose down and tips her eyes up to watch me. We all sleep then, for a bit, while the squirrels sort through the boxes overhead and the dog on the blanket keeps nervous watch.

I've called in tired to work. It's midmorning and I'm shuffling around in my long underwear, smoking cigarettes and drinking coffee. The whole house is bathed in sunlight and the faint odor of used diapers. The collie is on her blanket, taking one of her vampirish daytime naps. The other two dogs are being mild-mannered and charming. I nudge the collie with my foot.

"Wake up and smell zee bacons," I say. She startles awake, lifts her nose groggily, and falls back asleep. I get ready for the office.

"I'm leaving and I'm never coming back," I say while putting on my coat. I use my mother's aggrieved, underappreciated tone. The little brown dog wags her tail, transferring her gaze from me to the table, which is the last place she remembers seeing toast. The collie continues her ghoulish sleep, eyes partially open, teeth exposed, while the Labrador, who understands English, begins howling miserably. She wins the toast sweepstakes and is chewing loudly when I leave, the little dog barking ferociously at her.

Work is its usual comforting green-corridored self. There are three blinks on the answering machine, the first from an author who speaks very slowly, like a kindergarten teacher, asking about reprints. "What am I, the village idiot?" I ask the room, taking down his number in large backward characters. The second and third blinks are from my husband, the across-town apartment dweller.

The first makes my heart lurch in a hopeful way. "I have to talk to you right *now*," he says grimly. "Where *are* you? I can never find you."

"Try calling your own house," I say to the machine. In the second message he has composed himself.

"I'm *fine* now," he says firmly. "Disregard previous message and don't call me back, please; I have meetings." Click, dial tone, rewind.

I feel crestfallen, the leaping heart settles back into its hole in my chest. I say damn it out loud, just as Chris strides into the office.

"What?" he asks defensively. He tries to think if he's done anything wrong recently. He checks the table for work; none there. He's on top of it. We have a genial relationship these days, reading the paper together in the mornings, congratulating ourselves on each issue of the journal. It's a space physics quarterly and he's the editor and I'm the managing editor. I know nothing about the science part; my job is to shepherd the manuscripts through the review process and create a journal out of the acceptable ones.

Christoph Goertz. He's hip in a professorial kind of way, tall and lanky and white-haired, forty-seven years old, with an elegant trace of accent from his native Germany. He has a great dog, a giant black outlaw named Mica who runs through the streets of Iowa City at night, inspecting garbage. She's big and friendly but a bad judge of character and frequently runs right into the arms of the dog catcher. Chris is always bailing her out.

"They don't understand dogs," he says.

I spend more time with Chris than I ever did with my husband. The morning I told him I was being dumped he was genuinely perplexed.

"He's leaving *you?*" he asked.

Chris was drinking coffee, sitting at his table in front of the chalkboard. Behind his head was a chalk drawing of a hip, professorial man holding a coffee cup. It was a collaborative effort; I drew the man and Chris framed him, using brown chalk and a straightedge. The two-dimensional man and the three-dimensional man stared at me intently.

"He's leaving *you?*" And for an instant I saw myself from their vantage point across the room — Jo Ann — and a small bubble of self-esteem percolated up from the depths. Chris shrugged. "You'll do fine," he said.

During my current turmoils, I've come to think of work as my own kind of zen practice, the constant barrage of paper hypnotic and soothing. Chris lets me work an erratic, eccentric schedule, which gives me time to pursue my nonexistent writing career. In return I update his publications list for him and listen to stories about outer space.

Besides being an editor and a teacher, he's the head of a theoretical plasma physics team made up of graduate students and research scientists. During the summers he travels all over the world telling people about the magnetospheres of various planets, and when he comes back he brings me presents — a small bronze box from Africa with an alligator embossed on the top, a big piece of amber from Poland with the wings of flies preserved inside it, and, once, a set of delicate, horrifying bracelets made from the hide of an elephant.

Currently he is obsessed with the dust in the plasma of Saturn's rings. Plasma is the fourth state of matter. You've got your solid, your liquid, your gas, and then your plasma. In outer space there's the plasmasphere and the plasmapause. I like to avoid the math when I can and put a layperson's spin on these things.

"Plasma is blood," I told him.

"Exactly," he agreed, removing the comics page and handing it to me.

Mostly we have those kinds of conversations around the office, but today he's caught me at a weak moment, tucking my heart back inside my chest. I decide to be cavalier.

"I wish my *dog* was out tearing up the town and my *husband* was home peeing on a blanket," I say.

Chris thinks the dog thing has gone far enough. "Why are you letting this go on?" he asks solemnly.

"I'm not *letting* it, that's why," I tell him. There are stacks of manuscripts everywhere and he has all the pens over on his side of the room. "It just *is*, is all. Throw me a pen." He does, I miss it, stoop to pick it up, and when I straighten up again I might be crying.

You have control over this, he explains in his professor voice. You can decide how long she suffers.

This makes my heart pound. Absolutely not, I cannot do it. And then I weaken and say what I really want. For her to go to sleep and not wake up, just slip out of her skin and into the other world.

"Exactly," he says.

I have an ex–beauty queen coming over to get rid of the squirrels for me. She has long red hair and a smile that can stop trucks. I've seen her wrestle goats, scare off a giant snake, and express a dog's anal glands, all in one afternoon. I told her on the phone that a family of squirrels is living in the upstairs of my house and there's nothing I can do about it.

"They're making a monkey out of me," I said.

So Caroline climbs in her car and drives across half the state, pulls up in front of my house, and gets out carrying zucchinis, cigarettes, and a pair of big leather gloves. I'm sitting outside with my sweet old dog, who lurches to her feet, staggers three steps, sits down, and falls over. Caroline starts crying.

"Don't try to give me zucchini," I tell her.

We sit companionably on the front stoop for a while, staring at the dog and smoking cigarettes. One time I went to Caroline's house and she was nursing a dead cat that was still breathing. At some point that afternoon I saw her spoon baby food into its mouth and as soon as she turned away the whole pureed mess plopped back out. A day later she took it to the vet and had it euthanized. I remind her of this.

"You'll do it when you do it," she says firmly.

I pick the collie up like a fifty-pound bag of sticks and feathers, stagger inside, place her on the damp blankets, and put the other two nutcases in the backyard. From upstairs comes a crash and a shriek. Caroline stares up at the ceiling.

"It's like having the Wallendas stay at your house," I say cheerfully. All of a sudden I feel fond of the squirrels and fond of Caroline and fond of myself for heroically calling her to help me. The phone rings four times. It's the husband, and his voice over the answering machine sounds frantic. He pleads with whoever Jo Ann is to pick up the phone.

"Please? I think I might be freaking out," he says. "Am I ruining my life here, or what? Am I making a *mistake?* Jo?" He breathes raggedly and sniffs into the receiver for a moment, then hangs up with a muffled clatter.

Caroline stares at the machine like it's a copperhead.

"Holy fuckoly," she says, shaking her head. "You're *living* with this crap?"

"He wants me to reassure him that he's strong enough to leave me," I tell her. "Else he won't have fun on his bike ride. And guess what; I'm too tired to." Except that now I can see him in his dank little apartment, wringing his hands and staring out the windows. He's wearing his Sunday hairdo with a baseball cap trying to scrunch it down. In his rickety dresser is the new package of condoms he accidentally showed me last week.

Caroline lights another cigarette. The dog pees and thumps her tail.

I need to call him back because he's suffering.

"You call him back and I'm forced to kill you," Caroline says. She exhales smoke and points to the phone. "That is evil shit," she says.

I tend to agree. It's blanket time. I roll the collie off onto the floor and put the fresh ones down, roll her back. She stares at me with the face of love. I get her a treat, which she chews with gusto and then goes back to sleep. I carry the blankets down to the basement and stuff them into the machine, trudge back up the stairs. Caroline has finished smoking her medicine and is wearing the leather gloves which go all the way to her elbows. She's staring at the ceiling with determination.

The plan is that I'm supposed to separate one from the herd and get it in a corner. Caroline will take it from there. Unfortunately, my nerves are shot, and when I'm in the room with her and the squirrels are running around all I can do is scream. I'm not even afraid of them, but my screaming button is stuck on and the only way to turn it off is to leave the room.

"How are you doing?" I ask from the other side of the door. All I can hear is Caroline crashing around and swearing. Suddenly there is a high-pitched screech that doesn't end. The door opens and Caroline falls out into the hall, with a gray squirrel stuck to her glove. Brief pandemonium and then she clatters down the stairs and out the front door and returns looking triumphant.

The collie appears at the foot of the stairs with her head cocked and her ears up. She looks like a puppy for an instant, and then her feet start to slide. I run down and catch her and carry her upstairs so she can watch the show. They careen around the room, tearing the ancient wallpaper off the walls. The last one is a baby, so we keep it for a few minutes, looking at its little feet and its little tail. We show it to the collie, who stands up immediately and tries to get it.

Caroline patches the hole where they got in, cutting wood with a power saw down in the basement. She comes up wearing a toolbelt and lugging a ladder. I've seen a scrapbook of photos of her wearing evening gowns with a banner across her chest and a crown on her head. Curled hair, lipstick. She climbs down and puts the tools away. We eat nachos.

"I only make food that's boiled or melted these days," I tell her.

"I know," she replies.

We smoke cigarettes and think. The phone rings again but whoever it is hangs up.

"Is it him?" she asks.

"Nope."

The collie sleeps on her blankets while the other two dogs sit next to Caroline on the couch. She's looking through their ears for mites. At some point she gestures to the sleeping dog on the blanket and remarks that it seems like just two days ago she was a puppy.

"She was never a puppy," I say. "She's always been older than me."

When they say good-bye, she holds the collie's long nose in one hand and kisses her on the forehead; the collie stares back at her gravely. Caroline is crying when she leaves, a combination of squirrel adrenaline, and sadness. I cry, too, although I don't feel particularly bad about anything. I hand her the zucchini through the window and she pulls away from the curb.

The house is starting to get dark in that terrible early-evening twilit way. I turn on lights, get a cigarette, and go upstairs to the former squirrel room. The black dog comes with me and circles the room, snorting loudly, nose to floor. There is a spot of turmoil in an open box — they made a nest in some old disco shirts from the seventies. I suspect that's where the baby one slept. The mean landlady has evicted them.

Downstairs, I turn the lights back off and let evening have its way with me. Waves of pre-nighttime nervousness are coming from the collie's blanket. I sit next to her in the dimness, touching her ears, and listen for feet at the top of the stairs.

They're speaking in physics so I'm left out of the conversation. Chris apologetically erases one of the pictures I've drawn on the

blackboard and replaces it with a curving blue arrow surrounded by radiating chalk waves of green.

"If it's plasma, make it in red," I suggest helpfully. We're all
smoking illegally in the journal office with the door closed and
the window open. We're having a plasma party.

"We aren't discussing *plasma*," Bob says condescendingly.
He's smoking a horrendously smelly pipe. The longer he stays
in here the more it feels like I'm breathing small daggers in
through my nose. He and I don't get along; each of us thinks
the other needs to be taken down a peg. Once we had a hissing
match in the hallway which ended with him suggesting that I
could be fired, which drove me to tell him he was *already* fired,
and both of us stomped into our offices and slammed our
doors.

"I had to fire Bob," I tell Chris later.

"I heard," he says noncommittally. Bob is his best friend.
They spend at least half of each day standing in front of chalk-
boards, writing equations and arguing about outer space. Then
they write theoretical papers about what they come up with.
They're actually quite a big deal in the space physics commu-
nity, but around here they're just two guys who keep erasing
my pictures.

Someone knocks on the door and we put our cigarettes out.
Bob hides his pipe in the palm of his hand and opens the door.

It's Gang Lu, one of their students. Everyone lights up again.
Gang Lu stands stiffly talking to Chris while Bob holds a match
to his pipe and puffs fiercely; nose daggers waft up and out,
right in my direction. I give him a sugary smile and he gives me
one back. Unimaginable, really, that less than two months from
now one of his colleagues from abroad, a woman with delicate,
birdlike features, will appear at the door to my office and identify herself as a friend of Bob's. When she asks, I take her down
the hall to the room with the long table and then to his empty

office. I do this without saying anything because there's nothing to say, and she takes it all in with small, serious nods until the moment she sees his blackboard covered with scribbles and arrows and equations. At that point her face loosens and she starts to cry in long ragged sobs. An hour later I go back and the office is empty. When I erase the blackboard finally, I can see where she laid her hands carefully, where the numbers are ghostly and blurred.

Bob blows his smoke discreetly in my direction and waits for Chris to finish talking to Gang Lu, who is answering questions in a monotone — yes or no, or I don't know. Another Chinese student named Shan lets himself in after knocking lightly. He nods and smiles at me and then stands at a respectful distance, waiting to ask Chris a question.

It's like a physics conference in here. I wish they'd all leave so I could make my usual midafternoon spate of personal calls. I begin thumbing through papers in a businesslike way.

Bob pokes at his pipe with a bent paper clip. Shan yawns hugely and then looks embarrassed. Chris erases what he put on the blackboard and tries unsuccessfully to redraw my pecking parakeet. "I don't know how it goes," he says to me.

Gang Lu looks around the room idly with expressionless eyes. He's sick of physics and sick of the buffoons who practice it. The tall glacial German, Chris, who tells him what to do; the crass idiot Bob who talks to him like he is a dog; the student Shan whose ideas about plasma physics are treated with reverence and praised at every meeting. The woman who puts her feet on the desk and dismisses him with her eyes. Gang Lu no longer spends his evenings in the computer lab, running simulations and thinking about magnetic forces and invisible particles; he now spends them at the firing range, learning to hit a moving target with the gun he purchased last spring. He pictures himself holding the gun with both hands, arms straight out and steady; Clint Eastwood, only smarter. Clint Eastwood as a rocket scientist.

He stares at each person in turn, trying to gauge how much respect each of them has for him. One by one. Behind black-rimmed glasses, he counts with his eyes. In each case the verdict is clear: not enough.

— *jump*

The collie fell down the basement stairs. I don't know if she was disoriented and looking for me or what. But when I was at work she used her long nose like a lever and got the door to the basement open and tried to go down there except her legs wouldn't do it and she fell. I found her sleeping on the concrete floor in an unnatural position, one leg still awkwardly resting on the last step. I repositioned the leg and sat down next to her and petted her. We used to play a game called Maserati, where I'd grab her nose like a gearshift and put her through all the gears, first second third fourth, until we were going a hundred miles an hour through town. She thought it was funny.

Now I'm at work but this morning there's nothing to do, and every time I turn around I see her sprawled, eyes mute, leg bent upward. We're breaking each other's hearts. I draw a picture of her on the blackboard using brown chalk. I make *X*s where her eyes should be. Chris walks in with the morning paper and a cup of coffee. He looks around the clean office.

"Why are you here when there's no work to do?" he asks.

"I'm hiding from my life, what else," I tell him. This sounds perfectly reasonable to him. He gives me part of the paper.

His mother is visiting from Germany, a robust woman of eighty who is depressed and hoping to be cheered up. In the last year she has lost her one-hundred-year-old mother and her husband of sixty years. She mostly can't be cheered up, but she likes going to art galleries so Chris has been driving her around the Midwest, to our best cities, showing her what kind of art Americans like to look at.

"How's your mom?" I ask him.

He shrugs and makes a flat-handed so-so motion.

We read, smoke, drink coffee, and yawn. I decide to go home.

"Good idea," he says encouragingly.

It's November 1, 1991, the last day of the first part of my life. Before I leave I pick up the eraser and stand in front of the collie's picture on the blackboard, thinking. I can feel him watching me, drinking his coffee. He's wearing a gold shirt and blue jeans and a gray cardigan sweater. He is tall and lanky and white-haired, forty-seven years old. He has a wife named Ulrike, a daughter named Karein, and a son named Goran. A dog named Mica. A mother named Ursula. A friend named me.

I erase the *X*s.

Down the hall, Linhua Shan feeds numbers into a computer and watches as a graph is formed. The computer screen is brilliant blue, and the lines appear in red and yellow and green. Four keystrokes and the green becomes purple. More keystrokes and the blue background fades to the azure of a summer sky. The wave lines arc over it, crossing against one another. He asks the computer to print, and while it chugs along he pulls up a golf game on the screen and tees off.

One room over, at a desk, Gang Lu works on a letter to his sister in China. *The study of physics is more and more disappointing,* he tells her. *Modern physics is self-delusion* and *all my life I have been honest and straightforward, and I have most of all detested cunning, fawning sycophants and dishonest bureaucrats who think they are always right in everything.* Delicate Chinese characters all over a page. She was a kind and gentle sister, and he thanks her for that. He's going to kill himself. *You yourself should not be too sad about it, for at least I have found a few traveling companions to accompany me to the grave.* Inside the coat on the back of his chair are a .38-caliber handgun and a .22-caliber revolver. They're heavier than they look and weigh the pockets down. *My beloved elder sister, I take my eternal leave of you.*

The collie's eyes are almond-shaped; I draw them in with brown chalk and put a white bone next to her feet.

"That's better," Chris says kindly.

Before I leave the building I pass Gang Lu in the hallway and say hello. He has a letter in his hand and he's wearing his coat. He doesn't answer and I don't expect him to. At the end of the hallway are the double doors leading to the rest of my life. I push them open and walk through.

Friday afternoon seminar, everyone is glazed over, listening as someone explains something unexplainable at the head of the long table. Gang Lu stands up and leaves the room abruptly; goes down one floor to see if the chairman, Dwight, is sitting in his office. He is. The door is open. Gang Lu turns and walks back up the stairs and enters the meeting room again. Chris Goertz is sitting near the door and takes the first bullet in the back of the head. There is a loud popping sound and then blue smoke. Shan gets the second bullet in the forehead, the lenses of his glasses shatter. More smoke and the room rings with the popping. Bob Smith tries to crawl beneath the table. Gang Lu takes two steps, holds his arms straight out, and levels the gun with both hands. Bob looks up. The third bullet in the right hand, the fourth in the chest. Smoke. Elbows and legs, people trying to get out of the way and then out of the room.

Gang Lu walks quickly down the stairs, dispelling spent cartridges and loading new ones. From the doorway of Dwight's office: the fifth bullet in the head, the sixth strays, the seventh also in the head. A slumping. More smoke and ringing. Through the cloud an image comes forward — Bob Smith, hit in the chest, hit in the hand, still alive. Back up the stairs. Two scientists, young men, crouched over Bob, loosening his clothes, talking to him. From where he lies, Bob can see his best friend still sitting upright in a chair, head thrown back at an unnatural angle. Everything is broken and red. The two young scientists leave the room at gunpoint. Bob closes his eyes. The eighth and ninth bullets in his head. As Bob dies, Chris Goertz's body settles in his chair, a long sigh escapes his throat. Reload. Two more for Chris, one for Shan. Exit the building, cross two streets, run across the green, into building number two and upstairs.

The administrator, Anne Cleary, is summoned from her office by the receptionist. She speaks to him for a few seconds, he produces the gun and shoots her in the face. The receptionist, a young student working as a temp, is just beginning to stand when he shoots her in the mouth. He dispels the spent cartridges in the stairwell, loads new ones. Reaches the top of the steps, looks around. Is disoriented suddenly. The ringing and the smoke and the dissatisfaction of not checking all the names off the list. A slamming and a running sound, the shout of police. He walks into an empty classroom, takes off his coat, folds it carefully and puts it over the back of the chair. Checks his watch; twelve minutes since it began. Places the barrel against his right temple. Fires.

The first call comes at four o'clock. I'm reading on the bench in the kitchen, one foot on a sleeping dog's back. It's Mary, calling from work. There's been some kind of disturbance in the building, a rumor that Dwight was shot; cops are running through the halls carrying rifles. They're evacuating the building and she's coming over.

Dwight, a tall likable oddball who cut off his ponytail when they made him chair of the department. Greets everyone with a famous booming hello in the morning, studies plasma, just like Chris and Bob. Chris lives two and half blocks from the physics building; he'll be home by now if they've evacuated. I dial his house and his mother answers. She tells me that Chris won't be home until five o'clock, and then they're going to a play. Ulrike, her daughter-in-law, is coming back from a trip to Chicago and will join them. She wants to know why I'm looking for Chris; isn't he where I am?

No, I'm at home and I just had to ask him something. Could he please call me when he comes in.

She tells me that Chris showed her a drawing I made of him sitting at his desk behind a stack of manuscripts. She's so pleased to meet Chris's friends, and the Midwest is lovely, really, except it's very brown, isn't it?

It *is* very brown. We hang up.

The Midwest is very brown. The phone rings. It's a physicist. His wife, a friend of mine, is on the extension. Well, he's not sure, but it's possible that I should brace myself for bad news. I've already heard, I tell him, something happened to Dwight. There's a long pause and then his wife says, Jo Ann. It's possible that Chris was involved.

I think she means Chris shot Dwight. No, she says gently, killed too.

Mary is here. I tell them not to worry and hang up. I have two cigarettes going. Mary takes one and smokes it. She's not looking at me. I tell her about the phone call.

"They're out of it," I say. "They thought Chris was involved."

She repeats what they said: I think you should brace yourself for bad news. Pours whiskey in a coffee cup.

For a few minutes I can't sit down, I can't stand up. I can only smoke. The phone rings. Another physicist tells me there's some bad news. He mentions Chris and Bob and I tell him I don't want to talk right now. He says okay but to be prepared because it's going to be on the news any minute. It's 4:45.

"Now they're trying to stir Bob into the stew," I tell Mary. She nods; she's heard this, too. I have the distinct feeling there is something going on that I can either understand or not understand. There's a choice to be made.

"I don't understand," I tell Mary.

We sit in the darkening living room, smoking and sipping our cups of whiskey. Inside my head I keep thinking *Uh-oh,* over and over. I'm in a rattled condition; I can't calm down and figure this out.

"I think we should brace ourselves in case something bad has happened," I say to Mary. She nods. "Just in case. It won't hurt to be braced." She nods again. I realize that I don't know what *braced* means. You hear it all the time but that doesn't mean it makes sense. Whiskey is supposed to be bracing but what it is is awful. I want either tea or beer, no whiskey. Mary nods and heads into the kitchen.

Within an hour there are seven women in the dim living room, sitting. Switching back and forth between CNN and the special reports by the local news. There is something terrifying about the quality of the light and the way voices are echoing in the room. The phone never stops ringing, ever since the story hit the national news. Physics, University of Iowa, dead people. Names not yet released. Everyone I've ever known is checking in to see if I'm still alive. California calls, New York calls, Florida calls, Ohio calls twice. All the guests at a party my husband is having call, one after the other, to ask how I'm doing. Each time, fifty times, I think it might be Chris and then it isn't.

It occurs to me once that I could call his house and talk to him directly, find out exactly what happened. Fear that his mother would answer prevents me from doing it. By this time I am getting reconciled to the fact that Shan, Gang Lu, and Dwight were killed. Also an administrator and her office assistant. The Channel 9 newslady keeps saying there are six dead and two in critical condition. They're not saying who did the shooting. The names will be released at nine o'clock. Eventually I sacrifice all of them except Chris and Bob; they are the ones in critical condition, which is certainly not hopeless. At some point I go into the study to get away from the terrible dimness in the living room, all those eyes, all that calmness in the face of chaos. The collie tries to stand up but someone stops her with a handful of Fritos.

The study is small and cold after I shut the door, but more brightly lit than the living room. I can't remember what anything means. The phone rings and I pick up the extension and listen. My friend Michael is calling from Illinois for the second time. He asks Shirley if I'm holding up okay. Shirley says it's hard to tell. I go back into the living room.

The newslady breaks in at nine o'clock, and of course they drag it out as long as they can. I've already figured out that if they go in alphabetical order Chris will come first. Goertz, Lu, Nicholson, Shan, Smith. His name will come on first. She drones on, dead University of Iowa professors, lone gunman named Gang Lu.

Gang Lu. Lone gunman. Before I have a chance to absorb that she says, The dead are.

Chris's picture.

Oh no, oh God. I lean against Mary's chair and then leave the room abruptly. I have to stand in the bathroom for a while and look at myself in the mirror. I'm still Jo Ann, white face and dark hair. I have earrings on, tiny wrenches that hang from wires. In the living room she's pronouncing all the other names. The two critically wounded are the administrator and her assistant, Miya Sioson. The administrator is already dead for all practical purposes, although they won't disconnect the machines until the following afternoon. The student receptionist will survive but will never again be able to move more than her head. She was in Gang Lu's path and he shot her in the mouth and the bullet lodged in the top of her spine and not only will she never dance again, she'll never walk or write or spend a day alone. She got to keep her head but lost her body. The final victim is Chris's mother, who will weather it all with a dignified face and an erect spine, then return to Germany and kill herself without further words or fanfare.

I tell the white face in the mirror that Gang Lu did this, wrecked everything and killed all those people. It seems as ludicrous as everything else. I can't get my mind to work right, I'm still operating on yesterday's facts; today hasn't jelled yet. "It's a good thing none of this happened," I say to my face. A knock on the door and I open it.

The collie is swaying on her feet, toenails clenched to keep from sliding on the wood floor. Julene's hesitant face. "She wanted to come visit you," she tells me. I bring her in and close the door. We sit by the tub. She lifts her long nose to my face and I take her muzzle and we move through the gears slowly, first second third fourth, all the way through town, until what happened has happened and we know it has happened. We return to the living room. The second wave of calls is starting to come in, from those who just saw the faces on the news. Shirley screens. A knock comes on the door. Julene settles the dog down again on her blanket. It's the husband at the door, looking frantic. He hugs me hard but I'm made of cement, arms stuck in a down position.

The women immediately clear out, taking their leave, looking at the floor. Suddenly it's only me and him, sitting in our living room on a Friday night, just like always. I realize it took quite a bit of courage for him to come to the house when he did, facing all those women who think he's the Antichrist. The dogs are crowded against him on the couch and he's wearing a shirt I've never seen before. He's here to help me get through this. Me. He knows how awful this must be. Awful. He knows how I felt about Chris. Past tense. I have to put my hands over my face for a minute.

We sit silently in our living room. He watches the mute television screen and I watch him. The planes and ridges of his face are more familiar to me than my own. I understand that he wishes even more than I do that he still loved me. When he looks over at me, it's with an expression I've seen before. It's the way he looks at the dog on the blanket.

I get his coat and follow him out into the cold November night. There are stars and stars and stars. The sky is full of dead men, drifting in the blackness like helium balloons. My mother floats past in a hospital gown, trailing tubes. I go back inside where the heat is.

The house is empty and dim, full of dogs and cigarette butts. The collie has peed again. The television is flickering *Special Report* across the screen and I turn it off before the pictures appear. I bring blankets up, fresh and warm from the dryer.

After all the commotion the living room feels cavernous and dead. A branch scrapes against the house and for a brief instant I feel a surge of hope. They might have come back. And I stand at the foot of the stairs staring up into the darkness, listening for the sounds of their little squirrel feet. Silence. No matter how much you miss them. They never come back once they're gone.

I wake her up three times between midnight and dawn. She doesn't usually sleep this soundly but all the chaos and company in the house tonight have made her more tired than usual. The Lab wakes and drowsily begins licking her lower region. She stops and stares at me, trying to make out my face in the dark, then gives up and sleeps. The brown dog is flat on her back with her paws limp, wedged between me and the back of the couch.

I've propped myself so I'll be able to see when dawn starts to arrive. For now there are still planets and stars. Above the black branches of a maple is the dog star, Sirius, my personal favorite. The dusty rings of Saturn. Io, Jupiter's moon.

When I think I can't bear it for one more minute I reach down and nudge her gently with my dog-arm. She rises slowly, faltering, and stands over me in the darkness. My peer, my colleague. In a few hours the world will resume itself, but for now we're in a pocket of silence. We're in the plasmapause, a place of equilibrium, where the forces of the Earth meet the forces of the sun. I imagine it as a place of silence, where the particles of dust stop spinning and hang motionless in deep space.

Around my neck is the stone he brought me from Poland. I hold it out. *Like this?* I ask. Shards of fly wings, suspended in amber.

Exactly, he says.

Bulldozing the Baby

*A*t age three, my most successful relationship was with Hal, a boy doll. He had molded brown hair, a smiling vinyl face, and two outfits. One was actually his birthday suit, a stuffed body made of pink cloth with vinyl hands and feet attached. Clothes encumbered me; I liked the feeling of air on skin, and when left alone for more than five minutes, I'd routinely strip us down to our most basic outfits and we'd go outside to sit on the front stoop. Hal's other outfit was a plaid flannel shirt with pearl buttons and yellow pants with flannel cuffs. He had black feet molded in the shape of shoes.

The gorgeous thing about Hal was that not only was he my friend, he was also my slave. I made the majority of our decisions, including the bathtub one, which in retrospect was the beginning of the end. Our bath routine was like this: My mother would pick me up and stand me in the tub — I had fat, willful legs, and I wouldn't bend them while she was touching me — then while I was settling into the water and coordinating the bathtub toys, she'd undress Hal and sit him down on the toilet tank to watch me.

"Tell Jo-Jo she is *not* to stand up in the tub," she'd say to Hal, before leaving us to our own devices. I found it unnerving to have her speak directly to him; didn't she know he was a doll? Plus, Hal couldn't stop me from doing anything. The moment she left I'd stand up and sit back down whenever I felt like it. Hal's job was to watch.

The bathtub toys were dull in an indestructible kind of way. You could drown them or bounce them off the ceiling and they were still unbreakable plastic in primary colors. Hal, however, was both filthy and destructible; my mother had proved it by trying to scour his head with an S.O.S. pad — he now had a small bald patch on the crown of his head, just like a real guy.

I decided on impulse to bring Hal into the tub with me, just to see what would happen. First he floated, then when I pressed on his stomach he submerged, smiling placidly. It was at that exact moment that the spark went out of him — he became waterlogged in an unflattering way and all I could do was put him back up, dripping, on the toilet tank. He sat more slumpedly, and the pink cloth of his stuffed body had a gray cast to it. Something had gone wrong with my experiment.

My mother came in and tried to wash my hair. She'd given up reasoning with me long ago, had adopted a style that married brute force with loud comforting comments. "You're such a good girl," she lied, struggling to hold my head in the water. Soap was lapping onto my face. I shrieked and tried to shake my head; a wave washed over my mouth. "One more time and then we're done," she said resolutely, sitting me back up with one viselike hand and squirting soap on my head with the other. I looked her in the eye and shrieked again. My father came and stood in the door of the bathroom, watching.

"What're you doing to her?" he asked my mother.

"She's doing it to *me*," my mother replied grimly. She gestured with her head. "Look at Hal."

Crap. Now I'd have to listen to that. I stepped up my end of the struggle.

"Oh dear," my father said. Hal was collapsed on himself, dripping slightly. My father rolled him in a towel and wrung him a couple of times. I screamed; they were trying to kill us.

"*Shut up*," my mother said. She stood me up and began brass-knuckling my head with a towel. When she was done she swatted my wet rear. It made a loud insulting noise without exactly hurting. I collapsed on the bath mat, wailing, while she strode off to find my jammies.

The bathroom ceiling had sparkles on it. The dog-in-the-boat stain was still there. Hal was wadded up inside a towel on the floor. I unrolled him and we lay on the bath mat together, panting quietly. They had manhandled us.

My mother has hung Hal upside down on the clothesline. I'm spending the morning in the sandbox to be near him, using an old comb to make furrows and lines which I then plant blades of grass in. I'm making a farm. Every once in a while I use the comb on my own hair, and warm sand falls down the back of my shirt. Hal is watching from upside down, clothespins pinched into his calves, vinyl hands dangling near his ears.

"*I am not hurting him*," my mother said dangerously as she pinned him up there. I better not pull a trick like that again or somebody's in trouble. I try to reach the measuring cup and my leg makes the grass fall over. I have to stand up and stomp on it carefully and then sit back down and start over, combing in the rows. Once I find a caterpillar and hold it up to show Hal. He can't see too good upside down. The caterpillar won't get off my finger so I scrape it onto the sand and use my scoop to

throw it out on the ground, along with a considerable amount
of sand.

I have on blue sunglasses with wiener dogs on the frames. I
can pull up my shirt and fill my belly button with sand except
if I do she'll dig it out with the washcloth tonight. I'm starting
to learn cause and effect. Hal in the bathtub means Hal up in
the air. He still doesn't have his clothes on. I climb out of the
sandbox and sit down on the ground to take my sandals off. I
put my sunglasses on top of them and stand back up. After I
push my shorts and underwear down I have to sit again in order to pull them off my feet. The shirt gets stuck on my head
and I can't see. After a frantic second I get it off but it yanks
my nose. The barrettes slid out of my hair while the shirt was
going past; I put one inside each sandal. I get up and sit on the
edge of the sandbox to rest.

A bee is on the hollyhock by the fence. It steps into the
flower and walks around, then steps out again, flies to the
sandbox, and hangs in the air in front of my face, buzzing. I
shake my head at it and it hovers for another instant and then
takes off again, flies to Hal, and lights on his hanging hand.

Injury laid right over top of insult. I start screaming.

When she comes out we look at each other for a long moment, then she sighs, reaches up, releases the clothespins, lets
him drop, then catches him before he hits the ground. She
hands him over and stoops to collect my clothes while I put my
sunglasses back on. I follow her to the back door, carrying Hal
by the feet. His shoes are warm from the sun and he smiles as I
drag his face along through the grass and then — bump,
bump — up the two steps and into the house.

Hal's body has become lumpy, with protrusions of wadded
stuffing in some spots and absolutely nothing in others. My
mother tries to fix him each morning by squeezing him like a

tube of toothpaste, forcing the stuffing from his lower body into his upper body. A gritty, sandlike substance is coming through his pores. He's still smiling. Hal and I are the only ones who don't care about personal appearances.

"She tried to give him a bath," my mother tells my aunt, who is holding Hal and looking at him through the bottoms of her bifocals. They're trying to figure out if he can be given a torso transplant. My aunt runs her thumb over his bald spot.

"The paint's wearing off his head," she says definitively. "Throw him out and get her a new one." Thus spake Bernice.

"No," I say, shaking my head vigorously. I get right up in Aunt Bernie's face. I shake my head again, harder. She holds Hal out of my reach. I do one short bloodcurdling scream and she hands him over.

My mother, the one who is not taking credit for the bald spot on his head, lights a cigarette nervously and exhales. Bernie is the oldest of five brothers and sisters. My own big sister Linda is playing jacks on the kitchen floor and every time I move she calls out *She's getting my jacks.* My mother believes her. One more time and I'm going to be sat right down in a chair. Aunt Bernie is still waiting for a reply. Her eyebrows are in the middle of her forehead.

"Listen," my mother tells her. "She will scream until we're *all* in the asylum, you included." Bernie snorts, takes a cigarette and lights it. Smoke pours out her nose.

"She may run *you*," Bernie says dryly, "but she doesn't run *me*." Her own daughters are in the living room standing in separate corners. The crime was cursing. It's time for Hal's thumb to be sucked.

"She's got that thing in her *mouth*," Bernie says.

"Don't put that in your mouth," my mother tells me in a stagey, I'm-the-mother voice. I stare at her until she reaches over and gives his hand a yank. It doesn't move.

"She's *biting* on it," Bernie says.

"I don't know what's got into her today," my mother says nervously. She lights another cigarette and gives me a desperate glare. Linda's rubber ball bounces one, two, three, four times. Hal's hand drops back down to his side. "Okay then," my mother says.

When they put me down for my nap Bernie looks around the bedroom and says she doesn't know why they've got me in a crib. "It's either a crib or a leash," my mother says shortly. When they leave I cry the minimum amount and then put my feet through the bars. Hal is lying with his head on the pillow and the blanket up to his chin. I put him down at the bottom where he belongs and then I go down there with him. The ceiling is white and has sparkles just like in the bathroom. If I pee in this bed it doesn't matter but I don't have to pee right now. I put my face next to Hal's and close my eyes. The ceiling sparkles appear against my eyelids, like stars. Hal's got his arm under me.

In my sleep I show my girl cousins how to tie shoes, just like my dad showed me. Make a bunny, cross over, push one ear through, and pull. It's supposed to be a bow but it unravels, just like always. *I can't do it.* My girl cousins disappear and in their place is Bernice, who points to the corner. I shake my head. She takes the manual, grasp-and-steer approach. *This is not a good idea*, my mother whispers. I'm in the corner all alone and I can't feel Hal's arm in my back. Wherever I am, that's where Hal's supposed to be. I turn around and around, but the corner is completely empty. All that's in it is me.

Under the sofa: quite a bit of dirt, several jacks, a book called *The Wait for Me Kitten*, a ballpoint pen, and the crust off a peanut butter sandwich. No Hal. To look behind the refrigerator you have to put your cheek against the kitchen wall. All that's back there is dirt. The broom closet doesn't even have a broom in it, just the vacuum cleaner. Under Linda's bed are about ten sandwich crusts, a clear plastic coin purse with an empty lipstick tube inside, the usual dirt, and a strange piece of red felt that looks like the tongue of a stuffed animal. The bedroom closets yield nothing but shoes. Hal wouldn't be able to go out to the sandbox by himself because he can't walk. Nevertheless, I open the back screen door and call to him.

Nothing from Hal, but in the kitchen my mother drops what she's doing and moves directly to the telephone. She dials with a pencil, puts a cigarette in her mouth, fishes around in her pocket for a lighter, finds it, snaps it open, lights the cigarette, and says into the receiver Let me talk to your mom.

The kitchen counter can be gotten to by way of a red step stool; you can climb up there while your mother is in the other room and eat chocolate chips out of the cupboard. You can also stand in the sink and look at the whole backyard through the window. She stops me before I make it up to the counter. She's carrying the phone, the receiver pinned to her shoulder. The other arm picks me off the stool and sets me on the floor. I point to the cupboards.

"He's not up there," she says shortly.

She knows something.

Back in the living room I watch her as she finishes the call and hangs up. She leans back in her chair, lights another cigarette, and blows large ragged smoke rings up to the ceiling. Even when I lie down on the floor right at her feet she won't look at me. From upside down she doesn't resemble herself; she could be a lady from anywhere.

I gently kick the rungs of her chair, once, twice. Her eyes flicker downward for an instant, and then back up. She checks her watch, and then a second later checks it again.

Any minute now our menfolk should be coming home.

From the kitchen come the sounds of sizzling and whispering. Fried chicken and a mother and father. From outside, the rhythmic thump and scrape of a game of jacks being played on the front stoop. Linda and her best friend, Pattyann. In the living room is the sound of a thumb being sucked. My mother has brought out Petie, a stuffed dog with a missing tongue, to sit with me. We're on the sofa, being quiet and waiting. My mother peeks her head out of the kitchen and then summons my father.

"She's back to sucking her t-h-u-m," she says.

"B," my father tells her.

"What?" she says.

"There's a *b* on it," he explains.

"What did I say?" she asks.

"'T-h-u-m,'" he says.

"Either way," she answers.

She's wiping her hands on a dish towel and he's holding a spatula. They're looking at me. Two thumps, a scrape, and Linda tells Pattyann she's a cheater. I use my foot to move Petie down to the floor where he belongs. They consider me and I consider them. My mother is the first to fold.

"Jesus H.," she says, disappearing into the kitchen.

My father brings a pencil and a piece of paper over to the coffee table. We're going to draw pictures. I climb down off the couch and stand watching.

"You don't want to step on Petie, do you?" he asks me. Petie is underneath my feet.

I take the thumb out of my mouth and nod, then put it back in.

He draws a triangle with a beak. "That's a bird," he says, and offers me the pencil.

I can draw pretty hard as long as the pencil doesn't break. When I'm done the whole paper is covered with a picture, and the bird is nowhere in sight. My father licks one finger and rubs the extra pencil marks off the coffee table.

"Jo-Jo made a gorgeous picture," he calls to my mother. He considers it carefully, turning the paper sideways and then back.

"Is it a house?" he asks me. "Is it a dog? Is it Mommy?"

No, no, and no.

My mother comes in and stands over us. She looks at the picture and then at me.

"Hal?" she asks.

I take my thumb out just long enough to nod.

"This is truly unbelievable," my mother says. She's sitting in the rocking chair with her shoes off, smoking. My father is walking back and forth across the living room, singing. Each time he gets to the fringe on the rug he turns around and walks to the other fringe. The song is one he made up, called "Bye Oh Baby," and usually I hum along but not tonight. I can't actually cry anymore but I can still make the crying noise. He's patting me on the back and I'm patting him on the back. We're walking the floor with each other.

"She's a sandbag," he tells my mother as we go past.

"Tell me about it," she answers.

Linda appears suddenly, squinting in the light. She has her nightgown on backward and her hair is messed up from being asleep. She shields her eyes with one hand and stares at us all. "Can we have pancakes in the morning?" she asks the room.

"I'm going to pancake somebody right now," my mother says, preparing to stand up. Linda stomps back the way she came.

"I'd like to pancake *Bernice*," my father says darkly. He moves me to the other shoulder, turns, and walks. My hand is tired of patting, I'm just watching the rug go by. Three more times and he walks me over to the rocking chair and points me at my mother.

"She asleep?" he whispers.

My mother and I are looking at each other. "You asleep?" she asks.

I shake my head.

She sighs, stands up, goes to the telephone table, dials, and scratches her head with a pencil while she waits. "Wake up and smell the hysteria," she says into the receiver, and then carries the phone out to the kitchen. My father switches shoulders again and we sit down to rock.

When my mother comes back in she's carrying a bottle of beer. She's glad we're sitting down. Bernie and the monsters stopped at the Dairy Queen out on Route 50 to get ice cream cones on their way home.

"You *bet* they did," my father says, rocking. His shirt smells good.

There was no reason to cart the d-o-l-l in question all the way home, so he was placed in a t-r-a-s-h b-i-n at said Dairy Queen. Under the awning, next to the counter. That would have been approximately three o'clock, and it would be now, oh, twelve-thirty.

My father groans. "Shit," he says.

The chair is rocking and rocking.

My mother lifts her beer bottle by the neck and takes a sip. The chances are slim to none but maybe Roy Rogers should get on Trigger and ride out there. Dale Evans will stay here with her beer.

Rocking and rocking.

My eyes won't open, but I'm still wide-awake. I go back up in the air with my eyes closed and then down the hallway and to the right. My arms flop when he puts me down, but I'm not asleep. He leaves and comes back with Petie and I try to make the crying noise but nothing comes out.

After he closes the door, I struggle up just long enough to force Petie through the bars and onto the floor where he belongs.

"My pancakes have bonanas in them," Linda tells me. She's wearing shorts, a midriff top, and an Easter hat, pointing her fork at me. I'm sitting in the big-girl chair with a dish towel tied around me so I don't climb down. My pancakes are clean.

"Jo-Jo can have all the bananas she likes," my mother says. "But they don't interest her." She's drinking coffee and yawning, tapping a cigarette against her wrist. She can't find her lighter this morning.

"That's because her doll is gone and she misses him," Linda recites sadly. "Even though our dad went to find him he wasn't there because he probably went to the dump which we're all sad about but there's nothing we can do." She forks in a mouthful of pancake, chews thoughtfully, and swallows. "And now she keeps thinking, 'Where is my *doll*? Where is my *poor doll*? What will I *do* without my *doll*?'" She takes a long drink of milk and looks at my mother. "Right?"

"Right," my mother says dryly. She gets up and lights her cigarette using a burner on the stove. Linda starts to speak again, fork in the air, but she's halted with a look and a pointed finger.

I can't eat pancakes that don't taste good. I push the plate away and lean over as far as the dish towel will allow, put my cheek on the tablecloth, and close my eyes. Now they're gone and it's pure dark. My thumb tastes like syrup.

She's talking to her girlfriend on the phone and polishing the spoons at the same time. I'm sitting on the footstool which I've pushed in front of the picture window. Linda walks by on her way outside, carrying a plastic bowl which she holds way up in the air as she passes.

"I've got a norange," she tells me.

And I have a pop bead that rolled out from under the footstool. It fits perfectly in my nose but we're not doing that. I'm just holding it.

"You didn't ruin it," my mother says. "Fill it with water, put in a tablespoon cream of tartar, and then boil the hell out of it. You'll take all that black off there." She listens for a minute, polishing. "Well, you can be the bad housewife and I'll be the bad mother." She listens again. "Sitting at the window, staring out," she says in a low voice. "I don't know what to do next." More listening and then she laughs. I put my forehead and both my hands against the glass. Behind me is the sound of snapping fingers. She can snap her fingers so loud it scares you. I climb down off the footstool to get my bead and then climb back up again. She snaps again, twice, and I have to carry the bead over and deposit it in her hand. She puts it in the pocket of her pants and we stare at each other. "Maybe he ought to be cooking for *you*, since he's the big expert," she says. She feels my forehead, runs one hand quickly down the back of my shorts, turns me around, and points me at the stool. "I sprinkle potato chips over the top before I put it in," she says.

The front sidewalk has a hopscotch picture on it but Linda and Pattyann aren't out there. I don't know where a dump is, and I don't know how long it takes to get back from one. A car pulls up to the curb, stops, and one of my girl cousins gets out holding a sack. Aunt Bernie and my other cousin stay in the car.

My mother hangs up the phone and goes to the door while Bernice and I watch each other through the glass. "We went to the store and this is for Jo-Jo," my cousin says when she hands the sack over. She's been crying. "*We* didn't get anything!" she bursts out.

My mother sends her into the kitchen for cookies. "One for you, one for your sister, and none for your mom," she tells her. She holds up the sack and calls, "You didn't have to do this!" to Bernie, who rolls down her window.

"You're raising a brat!" she hollers.

My mother laughs and shakes her fist in the air. The girl cousin goes back down the sidewalk and triumphantly shows her mother the cookies before getting in. They pull away from the curb and my mother waves as they head down the street, then says, "I'd like to slap that mouth right off her face."

Linda and Pattyann come into view on the other side of the street. They look both ways and then hop across the street on one foot.

"I can't *wait* to see what's in here," my mother says brightly, setting the sack on the coffee table. She checks all her pockets, looking for her lighter, then puts a cigarette in her mouth and heads to the kitchen to light it on the stove.

They got that sack at the store. Outside, a lady is walking by with a dog, and Linda and Pattyann pet the dog so fervently the lady has to pull him away and keep going. The sack is folded over at the top and it's pretty big but not that big. Linda and Pattyann start playing hopscotch on the front sidewalk, using soda crackers for markers.

My mother is all excited about the sack. She sits down with her ashtray and pats the couch next to her. I climb up and then lie down with my eyes closed. She can't figure out why we aren't more curious about our new present. It must be something very special or they wouldn't have brought it all the way over here. You know, there just might be something inside that will make Jo-Jo forget her troubles. So. Is somebody ready to go down for her nap, or is she ready to *sit up here right now* and see what's in the sack?

It's a box with a picture of girl on it. She's wearing an apron over her dress and a pearl necklace. Her hair is curled and she has lipstick on. Inside the box are a broom, a dustpan, and a vacuum cleaner.

"Christ," my mother snorts. She puts her cigarette out, pulls me onto her lap, and rests her chin on my head. "Poor Jo-Jo," she says quietly.

They are miniature, and the vacuum cleaner has a pretend cord and a pretend knob to turn it on and off. The broom is yellow, the dustpan is pink, and the vacuum cleaner is orange with a pink-and-yellow-striped handle.

They're so glamorous I can barely look at them.

"She spent the whole afternoon cleaning under the beds," my mother tells my father. They're sharing a beer in the living room. My hair is wet from the bath and I have my cowgirl jammies on. Linda is in the bathtub now, singing a loud, monotonous song about not getting a new toy.

My mother is sewing a button on my father's shirt while he's still wearing it. "I was having this terrible feeling," she says, "that she'd be this forty-year-old woman, going around telling people that we took her d-o-l-l away from her." She leans down to bite off the thread.

My father tests his new button and it works perfectly. "In three days she won't remember she even *knew* that d-o-l-l," he predicts.

They stop talking and, in unison, lift their feet so I can vacuum under them.

The Family Hour

*I*f *she has to come up here we're* both going to regret it. It's ten o'clock at night and there has been a territorial dispute over where the line down the middle of the bed really is. After a short skirmish we have yelled downstairs to the mediator. From the top of the stairs all we can see is my father's bare feet crossed on the white divan and a corner of my mother's newspaper. They're drinking beer and eating popcorn. Linda pins my arms behind my back and I bite her. There are screaming noises.

She's had it. Once more and it's going to be the belt.

This surprises us and we tiptoe back into the bedroom. My mother's spanking abilities scare her and so she has a ratio of about one spank per forty threats. We always know where we happen to be along the spanking continuum. That's why we can't believe she's going straight for the belt. We're more afraid of her hand than the belt, because the belt is a cloth one from a housedress, while her hand is made of granite. But still, this is erratic behavior on her part, and we don't care for it.

Once we're back in the bedroom with the door closed, I say, "I'll give *her* the belt." Linda opens the door again and points her face down the hall toward the stairs.

"Mother?" she calls. "Jo Ann just said something you might want to hear."

There's a thud from downstairs and the sound of feet stomping. Linda slams the door shut and leaps for the bed; we hide under the covers, breathing into our nightgowns, but nothing happens. She faked us out.

The border dispute has to be settled with what is known as a foot-feet fight. This is where you lie on your back and put the soles of your feet against the soles of your sister's feet and then push with all your weak might until she gets tired of it and shoves you off the bed. There are rules to foot-feet fighting, but they are frequently defied, and then someone gets hurt, usually from being rocketed off the bed backward and onto the floor (me). On this occasion what goes wrong is that my own right foot slips from its station on her left foot and propels itself forward until it is stopped by her eye socket. She rolls herself up into a ball.

"That didn't hurt," I say immediately. She's got her head under a pillow, crying furiously and trying to kick me. I carefully get out of the way of her legs until she has me wadded up at the foot of the bed. Her sobs now have an alarming, forlorn quality, and it isn't like her to muffle them. I try a different approach: I start crying, too.

Eventually we fall asleep and roll as we always do into the demilitarized zone down the center of the bed. When I wake in the morning she's sitting in the rocking chair with her ankles crossed, virtuously reading her science book. I go back under the covers immediately. She has the most pronounced black eye I've ever seen, even on TV. I'm a dead man.

We dress ourselves slowly, not looking at one another; her underwear says Friday, mine says Wednesday, but today it doesn't matter who is right. White knee socks, navy blue knee socks, a gray skirt, a plaid one. Blouses. Teeth, faces, hair.

On the third step from the bottom we stop and look at ourselves in the hallway mirror. I've got my barrette in wrong. Linda has her mohair sweater buttoned over her shoulders like a cape, the way the girls in her class do it. Her face is thin on one side and fat on the other. The fat side is purple. I move slightly so that my own reflection goes into the bevel of the mirror, distorting my nose and one eye until I look like the monster that I am. It's time to sit down.

"Oh no you don't," she says firmly, lifting me by the collar of my shirt, steering me into the kitchen ahead of her. My mother is at the table, looking into a magnifying mirror, putting on makeup. A cigarette is going in the ashtray. My father is cracking our morning eggs into a bowl, dish towel tied around his waist, a spatula in his back pocket. He's singing the "I'm a Bum" song that drives my mother nuts. She's turning the radio up right at the moment we step into her line of view. The announcer makes a staticky squawk and then disappears into silence. My father sets his spoon down. My mother puts her glasses on.

Linda steps forward, Jo Ann steps backward.

I am immediately dispatched to the living room, where I can hear every word but not defend myself by looking stricken. In the kitchen my father whistles long and appreciatively until my mother tells him to shut up. "*Look* at this," she cries. I know just what she's doing: turning Linda's face back and forth, back and forth. I pick up some knitting from its basket and before I realize it I've unraveled a row and a half. My heart starts pounding. I'm a maniac, kicking people in the head and unraveling knitting.

"We *want* the truth," my mother says, in a voice that ensures she will never get it. A pause, an inhalation, an exhalation, and then the story unfolds. It has a complicated plot that is difficult but not impossible to follow, and several very dramatic things occur, but the gist is this: the bathroom doorknob poked her in the eye. It's a play with several acts but only one actress; my name is never mentioned. I hope he puts the eggs on pretty soon because I'm suddenly hungry. I begin fiddling with my barrette, trying to fix it.

"The doorknob would come up to about *here*," my mother says. I imagine she's pointing to my sister's stomach.

"Well, it didn't," Linda responds flatly. "It came up to *here*, as a matter of fact."

There is a long, stand-off silence in which all you can hear is Linda thinking.

"I had to pee so bad I was bending *over*," she says firmly. Brilliant. This is why she's the older sister and I'm the younger one.

Snap. Crack. My mother's lighter and my father's eggs. I don't see why I'm quarantined in the living room when I didn't do anything.

"Can someone please fix my bar*rette*?" I call out.

Right before we file out the door for school, my mother calls me over. She takes off her glasses to get a better bead on me. "Do *you* have any idea why your sister has a black eye?" she asks.

I hesitate. You hate to say it, but when it's the truth, it's the truth. She *never* looks where she's going.

In addition to Linda and me, there's a brother, a strange little guy named Bradley, obsessed with his own cowboy boots. He paces around and around the house, staring at his feet and humming the G.I. Joe song from the television commercial. He is the ringleader of a neighborhood gang of tiny boys, four-year-olds, who throw dirt and beat each other with sticks all day long. In the evenings he comes to dinner with an imaginary friend named Charcoal.

"Charcoal really needs a bath," my mother says, spooning Spaghettios onto his plate. His hands are perfectly clean right up to the wrists and the center of his face is cleared so we can see what he looks like. The rest of him is dirt.

"Charcoal was locked in the garage all day," he replies. My mother made fried chicken for dinner, but Brad will only eat food prepared by Chef Boyardee.

Across the table from me, Linda pushes a mouthful of potatoes past her teeth and lips until it's hanging there, making me sick. I will only eat potatoes in the form of french fries, and that's because I don't know that french fries *are* potatoes. I have a weak stomach. The second I open my mouth to complain, she sucks it back in and swallows, touches a napkin to her lips, and goes for a preemptive strike.

"Jo Ann is making me sick," she tells my mother. Everyone stops eating and looks at me. I'm searching my chicken leg for the big rubbery string. If I get that string in my mouth, dinner is over.

"I can't find it," I say. The fork won't do what I want it to, and chicken juice is getting on my hands. *Quit looking at me.* My mother reaches over and takes the chicken leg, drops it on my father's plate.

"Find the string for her," she tells him shortly. He looks at her, looks at the leg, and finally picks it up. He begins hacking at it amiably, gazing around the table in benign spirits. He's not paying attention to what he's supposed to be doing; the leg slips suddenly out of his grasp and, in the ensuing clatter, milk is dumped over and my father's plate is flooded.

banal

"Well, I'll be," he says slowly, watching with surprise as his beans and potatoes become islands. A full minute passes while we wait for my mother to do something about it. Eventually she gets up from the table, takes his plate, scrapes it into the dog's bowl, gets another plate from the cupboard and hurls some food onto it. While she's doing all this, my father is sitting with his elbows on the table and his face in his hands.

By the time she puts the new plate of food down in front of him, he's asleep. She shoves him and he comes to with a snort. He no longer has the amiable slap-happy look that offends her; now he looks belligerent. She tells him he's a sorry excuse for a man, which causes him to shrug.

"Who do you think you are?" she asks him. She has her face right up in his. "Dean Martin? Because he's nothing but a lush, too."

My father not only drinks like Dean Martin, but he actually looks like him. They sing alike, too, Dean on TV, and my father when he's shaving. He can't help but like Dean Martin, because they have so much in common. Somehow, though, the word lush hits him the wrong way and he guffaws instead of fighting back. My mother quickly corrects herself.

"He's a *drunk*," she says.

My father doesn't like that one bit. He tries to counter it by insulting Carol Burnett but my mother cuts him off. You don't see Carol Burnett standing there with a drink in her hand; she actually puts on a *show*. Usually I try to think of other things when they fight like this at the dinner table, like how to swallow. But by using television personalities, they're holding my interest. My favorite show is *That Girl*, but I'm one hundred percent sure they aren't going to mention her.

Linda ignores them completely, staring instead at me, willing me to look. I can see out of the corner of my eye what appears to be a Ping-Pong ball coming out of her mouth.

Next to me, Brad is a country unto himself, quietly stirring his Spaghettios and taking occasional peeks under the table at his cowboy boots. His mouth is orange.

Dinner ends when my father gets indignant and tries to stand up. He falls backward into the wall and the big ceramic salad fork drops from its hook and shatters. My mother can't have anything nice; the minute she gets something decent, it's ruined. She works all day and then comes home and makes a beautiful meal like this, and the dog is the only one who will eat it.

Soon there are distant unrestful snores coming from upstairs; from the sewing room the furious, intermittent buzz of the Singer 9000. In the living room, Brad and Charcoal play a friendly game of cards. "When I go like this, it means you lose," the visible one tells the invisible one.

This is our house in Moline, Illinois, a big white clapboard that needs new gutters. There's a little garage out back, and in the corner of the garage is an old cupboard. Inside it are cans of paint, folded rags, tools for cleaning fish, an old dog brush, and a bottle of vodka in a brown paper sack.

Here in the kitchen, African violets bloom wildly on the windowsill, hopped-up with fertilizer. The radio on the counter plays a new Beatles song and the girls take a break from clearing the table to clutch their hearts and listen. Tuesday night at the Beard household, and it's business as usual: Linda washes, Jo Ann dries.

interesting descript

Yimmer the dog is missing. She spends most of her time shedding on the furniture, or balanced on her back legs at the end of her chain, barking at the house. Right now, the last time any of us can remember seeing her was hours ago, at lunch, when she coughed up part of a garter snake on the living room rug.

My father is also missing, which has led the authorities — my mother and her girlfriend — to believe they are together.

"It isn't enough that he goes to the tavern in broad daylight," my mother says to Helen. Her mouth is full of pins. "He's got to advertise it to the neighbors." Popular thinking places Yimmer at the crime scene, a white dog against a brown brick establishment, fodder for local dinner table discussion tonight.

"If there's a garter snake in this neighborhood, then I'm moving," Helen tells her. They're making sheers for Helen's dining room, so she can open her drapes without the whole world looking in. They keep taking the pins out of their mouths in order to smoke, and then putting them back in. As soon as they get the hard part done they plan to switch from iced tea to beer.

All three kids have been dispatched to find the dog on our own block, but I have come back early, due to the bogus nature of the mission. We all know where she is. I'm trying to get my parakeet to look at me. No matter where I stand, next to his cage, he turns around in a single hopping motion and looks the other way.

"I think this bird is mad at me," I say. He wants me to put my finger in there so he can peck it. The back door slams and the refrigerator opens.

"Get out of there," my mother says through her pins.

Linda flops down on the sofa and opens her book, taking small bites off a radish. "She's putting her fingers in the birdcage," she tells my mother.

"I forgot," I say quickly.

"Well, he'll be happy to remind you," my mother says.

"Linda's eating a radish without washing it," I report.

"I wish I had about eight more just like them," my mother tells Helen. She goes to the back door and calls for Brad, very,

very loudly, in a voice designed to scare all neighborhood children, then stops at the refrigerator and gets two cans of beer.

It takes Brad a full ten minutes to report in, and when he does, it turns out he forgot his mission altogether and was making a campfire in the middle of the alley.

"We're rubbing the sticks together and then we're going to cook things over it," he tells my mother. His mouth is still vivid from lunch and he has his T-shirt on inside out. Helen is charmed by him and exclaims over the idea of a campfire in the alley. He glances at her. "Don't worry," he explains, "it's all pretend."

What about the dog?

"Huh?" he says.

The tavern is several long blocks away. The girls are to get their shoes on and go over there with the leash and see if the dog is waiting outside. If she is, they are to put the leash on her and bring her home. If it turns out they can do that without fighting, then they won't get beat to a pulp when they get back.

Helen thinks this is funny and so does my mother.

Two things we are never, under any circumstances, to do. Ride double on a bike and ride a bike on Nineteenth Avenue. Riding double means the person in control isn't, and if she ever catches one of her kids doing it, that's it for the bike; sold. Nineteenth Avenue is at the end of our street, a double-laned thoroughfare with no stoplights, lined with parked cars and carpeted with the pelts of squirrels and stray cats. We aren't even allowed to cross it on foot.

Linda's bike is new and almost too tall for her. We wheel it behind the garage and I climb on the back fender. I've got the dog leash wrapped conveniently around my neck. She gets on and we wobble for a distance, recover momentarily, and then fall over.

This time I sit on the handlebars, which is more comfortable, except Linda can't see around my head and if I shift my weight we swerve harshly. We veer past the campfire crew, who are sitting on the ground holding long sticks over a pile of short sticks; Brad's face is a blur of startlement, but he can be counted on to forget it as soon as we've crossed his line of vision. I'm balancing us by using my legs as rudders and keeping my head to the side so Linda can see where she's going.

Directly to Nineteenth Avenue and a right-hand swerve, out into the stream of Saturday afternoon cars. I bank my legs going around the turn and then am forced to retract them altogether, due to the close nature of the parked cars to my right and the whizzing cars to my left. Once my feet are settled on the front fender, I have to sit straight in order not to fall off, and once I sit straight, Linda can't see. Wobbling begins to occur almost immediately, along with shouting. I'm trying to tell her where to steer and she's trying to tell me she can't. Somebody's mother gets into the act by yelling at us out the window of a car going the other direction. Cars are honking and careening out around us, causing mayhem.

Up ahead there's a gap in the parked cars. A little street. I can't tell if she plans to take it or not, but I'm going for it. I bank my legs again and the traffic arcs out around us; Linda tries to compensate by leaning in the other direction. She uses her forehead to butt me between the shoulder blades.

No.

Yes.

Around the corner, clipping a parked car.

Sewer grate. *Here comes a sewer grate.*

Hard to describe how skinny my legs are, except to say that one of them fit perfectly down the sewer grate. I'm wearing the bike like a cape on my head and shoulders; Linda is in a heap with the wind knocked out of her. Her lips are moving but the sound is missing.

My leg is in the sewer.

One end of the handlebars is jammed into the grate and the front wheel, now curved like a potato chip, is pinning my head down. Six feet away, Nineteenth Avenue roars dynamically. Below the street, the air is cool and damp, like air-conditioning.

MY LEG IS IN THE SEWER.

Linda is up, making a bleating sound and circling her bike. Okay, she can't believe this. This is a practically *new* bike. This bike is now *ruined*. If it isn't ruined, you could've fooled *her*.

MY LEG IS IN THE SEWER.

She grabs the handlebar and tries to twist it out of the grate. When she lets go, my chin is pressed to the ground. I can now see the undercarriages of cars whizzing past, six feet away. The first one that decides to turn the corner will smash me like a garbage can lid. The direness of the situation dawns on both of us at the same moment. Linda steps discreetly onto the curb and starts walking backward.

DON'T LEAVE ME HERE.

"I'm not," she says, and then turns and starts running. She stops at the end of the block and begins limping, holding her elbows, until she's out of view.

This is more of an alley than an actual street, and the houses look like nobody's home. I try hollering as loud as I can, but Nineteenth Avenue drowns me out. Now my throat hurts. I'm going to be killed, and the only people I know in heaven are my grandfather and an old dog named Mike, who *got hit by a car*.

Help! Help! Help!

Nobody helps you when you need help. When your sister left you trapped in the sewer and your dad is at the tavern, drinking with the dog. Screaming doesn't work but I can't stop doing it. Nobody is helping me!

Oh, wait. Here they come. My mother and Helen, walking briskly, Linda hanging back a few paces, nursing herself. Helen points and suddenly my mother breaks into a run. I've never seen her run before! She gets larger and larger, her mouth a stark gash across her face, until she's just a pair of feet, the bike is wrenched out of the grate and thrown on the curb, I'm lifted, turned, and pulled. Up and out.

Well. That was easier than it looked.

Helen unwinds the leash from my neck, picks the gravel out of my shinbone, and tugs my shorts back around where they belong. She brushes the seat harder than she needs to, but I'm not in a position to say anything. My mother is sitting on the curb with her head on her knees, panting quietly and weeping.

Linda is just arriving on the scene. "Well, *that* was a close one," she says. "Just the kind of situation you read about, where a kid is riding her sister's bike and gets too close to Nineteenth Avenue." She's talking directly to Helen. My mother looks up.

"Get home," she says.

Linda is in for it.

"The both of you," she tells me.

We try to wheel the bike but it won't. Linda picks up the front end and I pick up the back end. At the end of the street we have to set it down for a second. My mother and Helen are still back there, sitting on the curb. My mother is talking and Helen is shaking her head.

My sewer leg is still cool to the touch. We pick up the bike and carry it another half block before resting. My mother and Helen are a ways behind, walking slowly.

"I think she's laughing," I tell Linda.

She sets down her end, fiddles with her shoelace, looks backward under her armpit, and then picks up the bike again. We resume walking. "I think she's crying."

She may be right. Either thing is possible.

We stow the bike in the garage for our dad to look at once he sobers up. Tomorrow, or a week from tomorrow, hard to say.

In the house, we divide up. I take a can of Pledge into the living room and start polishing the furniture; Linda runs dishwater and briskly begins dumping glasses and spoons into it. This place is a mess. My parakeet is asleep on his perch. I stick my finger through the bars and he's on it in an instant, biting into my knuckle with his beak. The door slams and I race back to my Pledge and spray it dramatically on the coffee table, all around the plastic flower arrangement.

Yimmer trots into the living room, leash trailing. She inspects the spot where she threw up earlier and then goes back into the kitchen for a long drink. My mother and Helen must have swung by the tavern on their way back. Well, that's a relief; one of the boozehounds is home.

The other one, lacking a leash, is always harder to retrieve.

I'm reading a book called *I Was Murdered*, a mysterious ghost story about a lady who can't rest until her killer is found. The cover has a picture of a typewriter, with two bloody hands typing the title on a piece of paper. I got it out of the neighbor's trash, along with some comic books that I already read. I'm partial to ghost stories, but this is nothing like the ones at the school library, where the ghosts invariably turn out to be real people guarding buried treasure. This book has a severed head in a refrigerator and other goings-on that I'm way too young to read about. That's the main reason I can't stop.

My sister is watching *The Man from U.N.C.L.E.* and putting on clear fingernail polish. She's quote babysitting unquote while my parents are over at the tavern. She made Brad go to bed a half hour ago but we can still hear him up there, punching his inflatable clown, which hits the floor and bobs back up again repeatedly. Sometimes he steps on the clown's head for a while to keep him down, and then there's silence. We don't care what he does, as long as he does it up there.

My book has me terrified. I want a bottle of pop really bad but it's in the refrigerator. I can picture it in there keeping a severed head company, blood dripping, pooling up on the Tupperware containers, seeping into the vegetable bin. My mother should watch me better and not let me read books like this, but if I do, my sister should go out to the refrigerator during a commercial and get my pop for me.

"Are you *kidding?*" she says, insulted.

This is grounds for a fight but before I can formulate my opening arguments, the sound of a key in the back door startles us both. *Man from U.N.C.L.E.* is followed by *Mission Impossible* is followed by *Creature Feature*. We're supposed to be able to watch all of them before our parents come home. It's getting so you can't count on anything around here.

My mother comes in and peruses the situation briefly, then listens at the stairs. Brad has fallen suddenly silent up there. I can tell by her face there won't be any *Creature Feature*, and popcorn is out of the question. Linda is watching her show intently, looking neither left nor right. I put my book down and watch it, too.

"This is a *great* show," I say to the room.

Out in the kitchen, my father is opening cupboards and getting spoons. When he opens the refrigerator there's a long moment of silence and then he shuts it again. I guess there was no head in there. A minute later he appears with ice cream, a bowl for Linda, a bowl for me, and a giant mixing bowl of it for himself. He joins us for the last fifteen minutes of *The Man from U.N.C.L.E.*, acting very impressed when Illya Kuryakin shoots a guy using his ballpoint pen for a gun. Yimmer is sitting on his lap.

"Is this the one where he has a telephone in his shoe?" he asks me.

"*Get Smart,*" I tell him. This confuses him for a moment and then he understands, and nods. It's been about two months since he's had a drink. Every night he sits in here while we watch TV, reading his bird books and talking to us. At first we didn't like it, but now we do.

My mother is in the kitchen alone, chipping the polish off her nails and smoking. I put the ice cream dishes in the sink and drift toward the refrigerator, where my bottle of pop is waiting.

"No you don't," she says curtly.

Nothing is fair around here. I can't decide whether to argue or not. The only light is coming from the living room, and she has her glasses off. Her eyes look weak and vulnerable, but her lips look like blades.

"He embarrassed me to death tonight," she says.

Uh-oh. Why did I come out here; what was I thinking?

"In front of everyone," she continues. "Embarrassed. To *death*."

She looks pretty alive to me, but if the truth be known, I've been embarrassed by him myself. Slumped and staggering, or sleeping all night in the passenger seat of the car, parked in the driveway, because he can't manage the back steps. Disappearing into the garage at odd times during the day, sipping from a sack and staring at the back of the house through the dark doorway, thinking no one can see him. We see him.

"There we all are," she says in a low voice. "Playing cards, trying to have *fun*, drinking a few cocktails, and he sits there for two hours drinking *orange juice*. Holier than thou; won't even have a drink on a Saturday night when we're at a *tavern*."

I think about this, standing on one foot. The dark kitchen, her cigarette going, the bitten-off words. It's hard to know what expression to put on my face. From the living room comes the sound of a fuse burning and then a theme song starts up.

"*Mission Impossible* is on," I tell her. She turns back to her ashtray and I return to the sofa. Linda is explaining the gist of the show to my dad.

"They all have different identities, and they have impossible missions," she tells him.

"I see," he says agreeably. "All different identities and missions."

"Impossible ones," she stresses.

"They aren't *impossible*, the people just think they are," I explain.

"They *seem* impossible, until the different-identity guys take over," he clarifies. "Is that it?"

We nod. He's drinking a glass of milk.

"Want me to get you a bottle of beer?" I ask him. Linda swivels her head around to stare at me but my dad keeps watching the television. After a minute he shakes his head no.

I want to go back to my book and leave them to their show, my mother to her dark kitchen, but I can't. My words are still hanging in the air of the living room, drowning out the TV. My dad is staring at *Mission Impossible* but he's no longer watching it.

Eventually, he shifts his weight and Yimmer stands up on his lap. She turns around and stares him in the face with her ears folded back and her tail going. He kisses her on the forehead, sets her on the floor, and stands up. Out to the kitchen. The refrigerator door opens, closes.

Yimmer's ears go up as she listens. Linda looks at me and I look at my book. Then the familiar, inevitable sound of a bottle being opened.

There's going to be a style show at school, something the PTA dreamed up. My mother is sewing three matching outfits and we have to be in it. Every time I think about it I feel sick; the dress she's making for me has the wrong kind of sleeves and she's threatening to give me a permanent. The last time she gave me a permanent only one side of it took, and I looked like I had a bush stuck to my head.

"You're not going to be in a style show with stringy hair," she tells me. She's working on a little shirt for Brad made of the same material as my dress and Linda's.

"Why don't you put puffy sleeves on *him* for a change?" I ask her. He's in the kitchen, eating a post-dinner bowl of cornflakes.

"No!" he calls out, alarmed.

"If I hear another word about sleeves, you won't *be* in a style show," she says to me.

"Sleeves," I reply.

Brad's in the doorway with a dripping spoon. She shows him his shirt with its long sleeves attached. It's getting cowboy fringe on the yoke. He goes back in the kitchen.

Linda is doing her homework at the same big table where my mother is sewing. Neither of them is interested in talking to me. The pattern for our dresses shows a picture of two girls, a younger one with short curly hair and puffy sleeves, an older one with long swingy hair and a little cape.

"You should make Linda wear this cape," I say to my mother. Linda looks up.

"You'll both have the cape," my mother says firmly.

A cape! Oh my God.

Linda starts poking herself in the head with the eraser on her pencil. She can't do her math and she's starting to get hysterical. My dad is the only one who can do math around here and we have no idea where he is. He didn't show up for dinner again, and it's a sore subject with my mother.

"Let me see," she tells Linda. This won't work. My mother can always get the answers but she figures it out in her head instead of on the paper. They make us figure it out on the paper to keep our parents from doing it for us at night when we're having hysterics.

"That's *old math*, Mother," Linda says desperately. "Do it in *new math*."

"Oh, *new math*," my mother says. "What a load of bullshit." She goes back to her sewing.

One time when Linda was three she shoved a tiny toy train up her nose to see how far it would go. It went quite a ways and she had to have it removed at the hospital. My mother has never gotten over this, and in our house, Life Savers and dry cleaning bags are treated like loaded handguns. So when Brad makes a choking noise out in the kitchen all hell breaks loose here in the dining room. My mother leaps up, throwing the shirt one way and the fringe the other, Linda drops her pencil, Yimmer barks.

Brad appears in the doorway, enormous-eyed. He points back to the kitchen with his spoon and then pushes past my mother into the living room where he turns and points again, then buries his shocked face in a sofa pillow. There's something in the kitchen! The rest of us crowd through the doorway to see.

Nothing.

My mother screams. I look around wildly and then I see it. Through the glass of the back door, framed by my grandmother's lace curtains, a face wearing a creature-feature mask. Black hair, forehead, two stunned eyes, and then the rest is blood. It looks like my dad. He fumbles for the doorknob but can't see through the mask, his hand slips and he cries out, something slides from his mouth and lands on his shirtfront; a wad of blood. My mother springs forward, opens the door, and we get the full picture. His clothes are frozen to his body and over it all, shirt, sport coat, trousers, is dark blood, coming from his mouth. Some of it is frozen and some of it is fresh. He can't move at all and when Linda and my mother try to pull him inside he groans and resists.

We get him up over the threshold, my mother on one side, Linda and me on the other, and then try to sit him in a chair in the middle of the kitchen. His legs won't bend. He groans again and then, with a noise like cracking ice, sits. My mother opens the oven door and turns it up to five hundred. She wants to look inside his mouth but he won't let her, so she gets a clean dish towel, wets it under the faucet, and starts wiping the blood from his face while Linda and I try to remove his shoes. The laces are stiff but the shoes come off okay. When we peel the socks away, his feet look like long yellow boats. My mother gasps when she sees them, then hands each of us a towel and tells us to rub. When we do, he makes the groaning noise again so we stop. She resituates him so he's closer to the oven, and then fills a dishpan with tepid water. When she sets his feet in it he makes a moaning sound.

Still working on his face, she tells me to go to the phone. I do. She tells me the number to dial and what to say. My aunt answers.

"It's Jo," I say.

"Well, hi Jo," she answers cheerfully.

"My mom needs you right now," I recite.

There is no pause. She's on her way. Twenty minutes.

The oven is blasting heat out into the kitchen. As my father thaws, the story comes out. It's hard to understand what he's saying, his words are slurred and when he talks blood dribbles out, over his chin and onto his soaked shirt. He wrecked the car.

Oh! my mother cries. The beautiful new Impala! Gold with gold interior!

He was drinking with Charlie at Silver's.

Silver's! Down in the west *end?* Silver's!

Left and started driving back, was coming around the viaduct, something happened.

The *viaduct!* At the slough? Clear down *there?* Oh my God!

She's walking in circles, frantic, stopping to clear the blood from his mouth. *The slough!* Linda is gone, somehow, it's only me in here with them.

Lost control and the car went down over the embankment into the water.

Into the *water?* Oh my dear goddamned *God!*

When he opened his eyes he was underwater and the window wouldn't roll down.

My mother is moaning and twisting the bloody dish towel.

He got it down finally and swam to shore, started walking, and came home.

You *walked?* From the *viaduct?* Five *miles?*

The kitchen is baking hot, but it's November outside. When I traipsed the four blocks to school this morning I had on my winter coat, a scarf, a hat, and mittens. And I was still cold. Suddenly my mother stops.

"Where's Charlie?" she asks him. Charlie is his drinking buddy.

He doesn't know.

Where is Charlie? Was he in the car?

He can't remember. My mother's face is stark white. Linda appears in the doorway. With her eyes on my father, she reaches out for me and we hold onto each other while my mother fumbles the phone book out of the drawer and begins clawing through it. She finds the number and dials. Someone answers.

"You S.O.B.," she says into the receiver and hangs up.

I guess he was home. The back door opens and my aunt comes in. When she sees my father she starts weeping with her hand over her mouth. Like everyone else, she's fond of my dad, she just wishes he would behave better. My mother tells her the story in terse words while my father dozes off, his head falling forward on his chest. He jerks awake and groans. Linda takes his feet out of the water and dries them.

"We love you, Dad," she whispers. He groans again as she tries to put dry socks on his poor feet. She stops and looks at me.

"We love you, Dad," I whisper. I help get the socks on and then we step back and wait until my aunt sends us into the living room. They're going to take him to the hospital.

From the sofa, arms around each other, we listen to the sounds from the kitchen, grunts and cries as they get him to his feet. My aunt appears in the doorway with her purse over her arm.

"Where's Brad?" she asks us.

Linda is mute. "Upstairs," I say.

"Jody, you go check on him," she tells me. "And I'll be back here as soon as we get your dad taken care of." She disappears again and there's a series of muffled cries as they ease him through the door and down the back steps. Linda and I each take our arms back and sit quietly, side by side on the sofa. Finally I have to speak.

"What was in his mouth?" I ask her.

"Everything but teeth," she replies.

His teeth are gone! His beautiful teeth that he smiles with.

The kitchen has to be cleaned up. There are bloody towels all over the floor and the oven is still blasting out heat. Linda will do that while I go upstairs to find Brad. She stands up wearily and doesn't move until I give her a push from behind. The steps go on and on forever until I'm finally at the top. The only light on upstairs is in the bathroom. Brad is in there, throwing up. I listen for a moment, until it's silent, and then push the door open. He's sitting on the floor next to the toilet, a dripping washcloth in his hand. I take it from him and wring it out. All around the toilet are chewed cornflakes and old Spaghettios.

"I can't find Charcoal!" he tells me. "He saw Dad and runned away!" I give the washcloth back and tell him to stay there, I'll go look for Charcoal.

I close the door behind me and stand for a moment in the dark upstairs hallway. I can hear Linda in the kitchen, moving things around, running water in the sink. In the morning, down at the slough, we'll watch them lift our gold Impala, dripping, from the icy water. By then we'll know that four of his ribs were broken on impact, and my mother will show us the terrible gouges on the steering wheel where his front teeth hit and were driven up into his head, behind his nose, perilously close to his brain. She'll tell us how the surgeon had to go in with a scalpel and remove them, one by one, while he thrashed, too drunk to be put under. His anesthesiologists were named Jack and Bud, she'll say grimly, drawing on her cigarette. Jack Daniel's and Budweiser.

I wait in the dark hall, counting to twenty, and then to fifty. I push the door open and go back in the bathroom.

"I found good old Charcoal," I say.

Brad looks up at me from his spot on the floor. He's been rubbing the washcloth across his brow and his hair is standing up in front. He stares at the air next to my shoulder for a moment, searching. Suddenly relief floods across his face.

"Hi," he says.

Waiting

He places himself in the gentle curve of the kidney-shaped desk. It is reddish mahogany, gleaming with Pledge and elbow grease. My sister can't take her eyes off the desk, because she's been looking for one like that at yard sales and estate sales and Saturday morning auctions for months. I, on the other hand, am captivated by the little guy sitting at the desk. He's in a somber profession, a low-voiced talker, a sympathizer, a crooning gentleman, here to make it all less of a hassle. He shuffles papers, twists the top of his thin gold pen and the ballpoint moves gently into place. He looks like he's been carefully dusted with talc — his head is bald and pink but it is not gleaming or garish in any way. Instead it has a matte surface, and the white hair around the bottom half of his head is straight and coarse. His shirt is white and the tips of the collar are crisp as notebook paper. Beneath his chin and above the snowy embankment of his shirtfront rides a bowtie, black with a pattern of small golden shields. It manages to be both pert and dignified, cheerful if you feel like being cheerful, or old-fashioned and somber if you're bummed.

Linda suddenly gets the hiccups and doesn't try to hide it. Each time she hiccups he touches his ear or clicks his gold pen. His earlobes are amazingly long and thick for such a little old man. Linda hiccups loudly and begins weeping. I give her the usual sympathetic glance and pat her hand, he gently leans forward and indicates with a gesture the box of tissues on the corner of the desk. She takes one and hiccups into her hand, subdued. She is over it already, I can tell. I try to catch her eye to point out the combed tufts emerging from his ears. He smiles a dim and sincere smile, finds the floor with his tiny feet, rises. He comes out from around the kidney-shaped desk and prepares his face for the task at hand. We move in behind him and trail down the carpeted hallway of the mansion, Linda noticing the wainscoting and chandeliers, me watching the back of his neck. He opens the door with a miniature flourish and moves back demurely. We step past him and into the room full of coffins.

The best ones are wood, rubbed to the sheen of the mahogany desk, lined with soft padding, intricate tucks and pleats and folds. All that effort. Linda runs her hand along the surface of one, pokes the satin pillow delicately with one finger. It has the kind of brass handles you find on an old-fashioned sideboard. "This one looks like a yacht," she remarks.

I glance at Mr. Larson but he's looking studiously at the tips of his shoes, rocking himself gently forward and backward, waiting. Somewhere deep within the house something flushes, long tubes feed fluids into and out of stiffening lumps.

"I can't do this," I tell them. He reaches behind the door for a folding chair and as he pulls it out the seat falls smoothly into place with a satisfying click. I sit down while Mr. Larson pads down the hall to get me a glass of water. He is accommodating and resourceful but clearly unimpressed, like a plumber in the presence of a medium clog. While he's gone Linda takes my hair in her hands and winds it softly, lets it drop. She points to the hull of a metal-sided casket.

"I like that one," she says. She wanders over and peers inside, touches the lid. She turns after a moment. "Can you keep doing this or do you need to leave?"

I shrug. Better now than later, which could end up being Christmas morning. The casket she's touching looks like the *Titanic*, gunmetal gray, waiting to be launched.

"What a waste, don't you think? All those gorgeous trees being chopped down just to get planted all over again," she said. "Here comes your guy."

He crouches to hand me the cup of water, hands on knees, wrinkled-up brow. It tastes like water from a bathroom sink.

"We think we might get her a metal one," I tell him, rising. "We like the wooden ones but they're too nice to put in the ground." I look to Linda and she nods in support.

"Plus," she says, "you know." She thinks for a second while we wait and then it comes back to her. "They go in a *vault*," she finishes. "So who cares." She looks at him probingly. Her eyes have soft blue pouches underneath and she's getting a dangerous air about her.

"We have to get going anyway," I tell him. "We have to get back before she wonders where we are."

In her hospital bed, bent like a branch against the pain, she watches the clock, anticipates the arrival of a daughter. *Where have you been?* Her voice vanished three days ago, leaving eyes and hands for communicating. *I've been here all alone, no one would stay in the room with me, you're the only one and you left.* This is my shift alone with her. The afternoon pulls itself along.

On the rolling lunch tray is a plate of Christmas cookies decorated with glaring Santas and crooked reindeer shapes. One kind has maroon jelly poured into a reservoir in the center and I take a small bite. I have a thing about red jelly but creaky old Velma Edwards made it so I'm willing to give it a shot. Ready, aim, it lands with a crumbling thud in the wastebasket. My mother rolls her gray, diminishing eyes and gives an invisible smirk. Linda has eaten almost all the good ones, left the jelly and green sugar for me. *Where did you girls go?* She has a clear tube poked up her nose nowadays, connected to an oxygen tank like an astronaut prepared to leave the ship. There is absolute silence, the clank and squeak of the hospital giving way for a moment as an angel passes over, wings beating. The instant passes and the hospital resumes itself, a cart bumps, a nurse calls out loudly, rudely, somewhere down the hall. In the room Coke seethes as I pour it into a glass. *Where did you girls go? Why did both of you need to go at once, leaving me here by myself?* I get a picture of her long ago, shopping, eating lunch in the mezzanine at McCabe's, picking out school clothes. Tall and thin in a beautiful suit; lemon meringue pie and coffee. The slide changes and the tufted ears of tiny Mr. Larson click into view. *Why did both of you have to go at once?* I rise to the occasion. Now-now, I point out, it's awful close to Christmas to be asking those kinds of questions.

Her eyes move past me, over my head, and I feel suddenly the tepid breath of Barnelle. He's a swashbuckler today, actually wearing one of those head things, like a doctor in the movies. It is a flat metallic disk connected to a band and he lifts it off and shoves it into the pocket of his suitcoat. The hair over the top of his head is a delicate auburn doily. He pats it down, using the palm of his hand, pushing the tattered strands back in place, willing them to stay there. He's wearing a plastic Santa Claus face on his lapel. He smiles at her, he has always acted as though he loves her and regrets this. He acknowledges me with a tilt of the head, some kind of invisible language that works, lifts her wrist and counts the pulse, corpuscles stepping through from her hand to her arm, one by one, like soldiers heading back to camp. He finishes and says Hello, girls in a sweet, cheerful voice and then pulls the string on his Santa Claus. The nose lights up and beams across the bedcovers. Barnelle is sending us a signal, Santa's nose twinkling like Mars. It's four o'clock and I'm ready to do something else for a while. My legs want to walk, my eyes keep finding the window.

"I saw Barn-door," Linda announces. She is back, ready for her shift, standing in the doorway with snow melting on her coat collar. "He was climbing into his gold-plated Cadillac, hightailing it home." Linda hates Barnelle with a rare enthusiasm, able to tick off his crimes on the fingers of both hands. She passes the plate where the rejected Christmas cookies used to be. "God, you'll eat *anything*," she remarks cheerfully. She's leaving tracks all over the clean floor, in meandering circles. She's been wrapping Christmas presents for her kids, I know, and her eyes look better. She crinkles them at me sympathetically. "Was Barn-door open?" she asks. This is rhetorical. Over on the bed the gray eyes are closed. Linda wants to know how it's going, how she's doing, but the eyes might open again unexpectedly. We tiptoe out.

"I stopped at home and went through her closet," Linda tells me. Nowadays she and I speak of the house where we grew up as home, we forget for long hours the places we live now, which have cupboards with our spices and canned peas, dressers with our clothes. When an aunt or our brother relieves us at the hospital we drive over there for some empty time, some quiet, and sit at her kitchen table with the carvings of childhood forks in its surface, stand drinking coffee right on the worn spot where she stood to stuff chickens, weave the crusts on pies. Home, we say to each other, drawing those dented walls around us like a wool blanket, two little girls in matching nightgowns, pinching and elbowing, acting hateful, getting yelled at. She was browsing, trying to find something to bury her in.

I stretch and yawn, shake it off, tell her about Barnelle's Santa.

"Gawd," she drawls. "Did he let on when or anything?" She squints when she asks this, afraid to know, afraid not to. Barnelle has predicted two days, which will land us right smack on Christmas. We have told each other ironically, Why not? and marvel at how the universe is dribbling us like a basketball and then shooting us into the air.

"He couldn't," I tell her, "because she was alert. And I couldn't follow him out because she already got on me about leaving with you this morning. She wanted to know where we went." We both shiver at that and then in turn begin crying, the ugly kind, where you turn your clenched face to the wall until it passes. A nurse comes forward, silent, and touches our shoulders. This nurse told me yesterday she hadn't finished her shopping, still had crowds and the hectic traffic at the mall to contend with. Last week, when she could sit upright and talk a little, my mother had given me her wedding ring for Christmas.

There is slush and cold air all up and down the hall. When I go back in to get my coat her eyes are open, talking even though no one can hear. *You girls left me again.* Linda is behind me, getting her needlepoint out, untangling skeins of bright yarn. I pull on my gloves slowly, pushing each finger down meticulously, getting my keys ready for the cold, avoiding her eyes. Behind me Linda says, Hey, remembering something. She digs around in her coat pocket.

"Look, Ma," she says softly, moving toward the bed. I step backward into the doorway, halfway gone. Linda holds a sprig of plastic mistletoe in the air above my mother's head. She whispers something I can't hear and bends down. I'm gone.

Suddenly I have this notion that she needs to wear flannel against her skin. I stop at a department store and join the current of tinkling people, Christmas shoppers. Music rains down and a clerk comes forward to ask if she can help. She has lost the heel to one pump and is trying to compensate by walking on tiptoe with that foot. She leads me to lingerie and begins thumbing patiently through nightgowns on a rack, showing me things. I tell her that it needs to be worn beneath a blouse. This confuses her and she thinks wearily for a second, one finger to her lip, one heel up in thin air. She produces an expensive long-underwear shirt made of raw silk, a tiny pink satin flower on the scooped neckline. I buy it even though I'm not sure anymore why I'm here, what I'm doing. I decide I might as well go back, only two days left.

I run into Barnelle in the main lobby, he's got his small son with him. I feel bad that he can't get any rest, can't be left alone for five minutes. He speaks frankly to me while his son attempts to tie his shoes together. He says quite honestly that he has gotten very attached to her and I say I have too, actually. He hugs me then, hard, his arms like a big pair of forceps. He lets go and one hand scans his head, searching out the wandering hairs, laying them flat. I've seen him on a bench before, reading X rays and shaking his head, biting his nails. He bends down now and unties the laces before he takes a step, his son disappointed but philosophical. There are Christmas presents waiting at home.

The room is darkening, Linda is asleep in the chair, knees drawn up like a shield, hands circling her stockinged feet. I can't tell what's happening on the bed until I turn on the light.

Her eyes are opened wide, frightened, helpless. *You left me, you girls, and here I am in the dark!* Darkness has a personality now, a power. I understand this very well, quilted satin pressing down in the velvet blackness, brushing the nose, the face. I turn on all the lights but Linda continues to sleep soundly until I bump her chair with my foot. She stretches her legs out and groans, gives me a dirty look, and I give her one back. I hold two fingers up to remind her of how much longer she needs to keep this up, to pay attention. She holds up one finger, guess which one, to remind me of who's the oldest, who's the boss. I would love more than anything to slap her.

I go to the cafeteria for a strawberry shake instead, which I can eat in front of her. On the way back up I land in an elevator with ten Christmas carolers. They seem like churchy types, the men are all shaved within an inch of their lives and the women look good-natured and opinionated. Two of them are quietly trying to harmonize on something I've never heard before, something Latin-sounding and mournful. A couple others practice scales and end up sounding out of tune. They get out on my floor and consult a list, everyone trying to get his or her head in there and direct the way. They end up following me, trying to stay a few paces behind. They are going where I'm going.

I close the door behind me and motion my sister over, whisper to her while the eyes on the bed try to make out what I'm saying. Quietly behind me, behind the oak of the door, their voices join together, hesitantly at first and then, gaining momentum, confidently. They are taking care to remember they are in a hospital, there are sick people here, but they love these songs, I can tell. One of the guys has a lilting baritone and one of the women a high vibrato. Linda hesitates and then opens the door, gestures for them to step in. We move to the head of the bed and stand like cops with our arms folded, trying to

smile. They finish one song and all look expectantly at the
lady with the vibrato. She says, Three, and they begin to sing
"White Christmas." This is our mother's favorite, she used to
put Bing Crosby on the turntable when we all sat down for
Christmas Eve dinner. It was part of the feast, like the white
candles, the clean linen tablecloth, the gleaming china. As she
passed the first bowl and our father stood to carve they would
sing it together, one at each end of the table, softly serenading
their children. Our father, in fact, had a wonderful strong baritone just like someone in the crowd of carolers. Suddenly regret is swelling in the room like the voices of the choir. As she
lies in the bed she weeps, for Bing, for the melting, shimmering candles, the filigree on the holiday tablecloth. She is an un-
willing astronaut, bumping against the thick glass of the ship,
her line tangling lazily in zero gravity, face mask fogged with
fear. My sister reaches across, over the bed, and we both em-
brace the mother, holding her on earth, pulling her onto the
ship, breathing our oxygen into her line. Ten hours later she is
dead.

Oh God, it is bitterly cold. The snow is crusted over into
shocked mounds, hard as Styrofoam. My fingers are burning
twigs inside my gloves, my toes ache like amputations. The
heater fan in Linda's car screamed until we had to turn it off
and give ourselves over to the freezing-freezing cold. Old man
Larson is offering something warm in delicate cups. My poor
fingers. It is morning now and he is drinking his own cup of
something hot. I guess it's coffee, although I can almost see
through to the bottom of the cup. He tips the cup to his little-
guy lips but refrains from raising a pinky — he couldn't care
less about cheering me up. He's in the morning-after mode
right now; he's not looking directly at either of us and he has

cleared his throat several hollow times. Linda sits up straighter and visibly tries to pay better attention. She shakes her head and clears her own throat one, two, three times in a row. Now Larson is glaring at her, his eyes vivid blue on a yellow background.

I look away. I can feel her gazing at my ear. I look back. Then she winks and he sees and now it's even more tense.

We have selected the *Titanic* with ivory satin and the vault with the million-year guarantee of no seepage. He has accepted with grace both the outfit we've brought on a wire hanger and the prescription bottle full of safety pins, all sizes, that we think he'll need to make her clothes fit her now. Linda thought he probably had special clamps for that sort of thing but we decided it would be better if he used the safety pins from her junk drawer. He looked at them for a long second and then set them on the corner of the kidney-shaped desk. I've given up on the long-underwear idea. Actually, I'm wearing it myself because of how cold it is outside.

In a brown paper sack sitting next to my chair, between Linda and me, is her wig. We hate to give it over, both of us have held it in our laps at different times during the last few hours. It is too morbid, though, even for us. She takes it out of the bag quickly and shows it to Larson, puts it back in. She told me in the car she was going to try and scare him with it, but I guess she changed her mind.

He informs us that the flowers have started to arrive, invites us to come back and see how they have begun to arrange them on stands and in clusters. We rise and leave the pale gray suit on its hanger, the wig crouching in its sack, the bottle of pins from the top left kitchen drawer. My sister touches the mahogany desk like it's a tree in the forest. As we match his tiny steps down the wainscoted hall we have no idea, at this minute, that he is an artist, a gentleman. We have no idea as we move toward the scent of the flowers and the Christmas greens that he will continue on through his beautiful house, leaving us behind to read cards and talk. He will go through two more rooms, down a set of stairs to a place where she lies. While we linger, rubbing our hands and whispering to each other, the grandson who is minding us watches the wall and chews gum. At this moment we don't know that downstairs he is working magic, that he will present to us a woman who looks rested.

That's how I will get to see her last, in her pale gray wool suit and pink blouse, her glasses resting on her nose as though she's just dropped off for a minute; her cheeks will be okay again. The clothes will fit perfectly, as though she hadn't lost a pound. Before the crowd arrives, when it's just me and my sister and an aunt, he will reach in his pocket and bring forth the bottle of pins, half gone.

Her hands are the only wrong thing. They look strange to me and I can't figure out why until Linda picks up my hand and shows me: Her wedding ring is on my finger; I forgot she gave it to me. The hands begin to look more normal to me now, and the silence of the room gives way to the breathing of the sisters, the coldness of the kissed hands, and the empty air that says *You girls, you girls.*

Out There

*I*t *isn't even eight* A.M. *and I'm hot.*
My rear end is welded to the seat just like it was yesterday. I'm
fifty miles from the motel and about a thousand and a half from
home, in a little white Mazda with 140,000 miles on it and no
rust. I'm all alone in Alabama, with only a cooler and a tape
deck for company. It's already in the high 80s. Yesterday, coming up from the keys through Florida, I had a day-long anxiety
attack that I decided last night was really heat prostration. I
was a cinder with a brain; I was actually whimpering. I kept
thinking I saw alligators at the edge of the highway.

There were about four hundred exploded armadillos, too,
but I got used to them. They were real, and real dead. The alligators weren't real or dead, but they may have been after me.
I'm running away from running away from home.

I bolted four weeks ago, leaving my husband to tend the

dogs and tool around town on his bicycle. He doesn't love me anymore, it's both trite and true. He does love himself, though. He's begun wearing cologne and staring into the mirror for long minutes, trying out smiles. He's become a politician. After thirteen years he came to realize that the more successful he got, the less he loved me. That's how he put it, late one night. He won that screaming match. He said, gently and sadly, "I feel sort of embarrassed of you."

I said, "Of what? The way I look? The way I act?"

And he said, softly, "Everything, sort of."

And it was true. Well, I decided to take a trip to Florida. I sat on my haunches in Key West for four weeks, writing and seething and striking up conversations with strangers. I had my thirty-fifth birthday there, weeping into a basket of shrimp. I drank beer and had long involved dreams about cigarettes, I wrote nearly fifty pages on my novel. It's in my trunk at this very moment, dead and decomposing. Boy, do I need a cup of coffee.

There's not much happening this early in the morning. The highway looks interminable again. So far, no alligators. I have a box of seashells in my back seat and I reach back and get a fluted one, pale gray with a pearly interior, to put on the dashboard. I can do everything while I'm driving. At the end of this trip I will have driven 3,999 miles all alone, me and the windshield, me and the radio, me and the creepy alligators. Don't ask me why I didn't get that last mile in, driving around the block a few times or getting a tiny bit lost once. I didn't though, and there you have it. Four thousand sounds like a lot more than 3,999 does; I feel sort of embarrassed for myself.

My window is broken, the crank fell off in Tallahassee on the way down. In order to roll it up or down I have to put the crank back on and turn it slowly and carefully, using one hand to push up the glass. So, mostly I leave it down. I baked like a biscuit yesterday, my left arm is so brown it looks like a branch. Today I'm wearing a long-sleeved white shirt to protect myself. I compromised on wearing long sleeves by going naked underneath it. It's actually cooler this way, compared to yesterday when I drove in my swimming suit top with my hair stuck up like a fountain on top of my head. Plus, I'm having a nervous breakdown. I've got that wild-eyed look.

A little four-lane blacktop running through the Alabama countryside, that's what I'm on. It's pretty, too, better than Florida, which was billboards and condos built on old dump sites. This is like driving between rolling emerald carpets. You can't see the two lanes going in the opposite direction because there's a screen of trees. I'm starting to get in a good mood again. The best was Georgia, coming down. Willow trees and red dirt and snakes stretched out alongside the road. I kept thinking, That looks like a *rope,* and then it would be a huge snake. A few miles later I would think, That looks like a *snake,* and it would be some snarl of something dropped off a truck.

Little convenience store, stuck out in the middle of nothing, a stain on the carpet. I'm gassing it up, getting some coffee. My white shirt is gaping open and I have nothing on underneath it, but who cares, I'll never see these people again. What do I care what Alabama thinks about me. This is a new and unusual attitude for me. I'm practicing being snotty, in anticipation of being dumped by my husband when I get back to Iowa.

I swagger from the gas pump to the store, I don't even care if my boobs are roaming around inside my shirt, if my hair is a freaky snarl, if I look defiant and uppity. There's nothing to be embarrassed of. I bring my coffee cup along and fill it at the counter. Various men, oldish and grungy, sit at tables eating eggs with wadded-up toast. They stare at me carefully while they chew. I ignore them and pay the woman at the counter. She's smoking a cigarette so I envy her.

"Great day, huh?" I ask her. She counts out my change.

"It is, honey," she says. She reaches for her cigarette and takes a puff, blows it up above my head. "Wish I wudn't in *here*."

"Well, it's getting hotter by the minute," I tell her. I've adopted an accent in just four weeks, an intermittent drawl that makes me think I'm not who everyone thinks I am.

"Y'all think this's hot?" she says idly. "*This* ain't hot."

When I leave, the men are still staring at me in a sullen way. I get in, rearrange all my junk so I have everything handy that I need, choose a Neil Young tape and pop it in the deck, fasten the belt, and then move back out on the highway. Back to the emerald carpet and the road home. Iowa is creeping toward me like a panther.

All I do is sing when I drive. Sing and drink: coffee, Coke, water, juice, coffee. And think. I sing and drink and think. On the way down I would sing, drink, think, and weep uncontrollably, but I'm past that now. Now I suffer bouts of free-floating hostility, which is much better. I plan to use it when I get home.

A car swings up alongside me so I pause in my singing until it goes past. People who sing in their cars always cheer me up, but I'd rather not be caught doing it. On the road, we're all singing, picking our noses, embarrassing ourselves wildly; it gets tiresome. I pause and hum, but the car sticks alongside me so I glance over. It's a guy. He grins and makes a lewd gesture with his mouth. I don't even want to say what it is, it's that disgusting. Tongue darting in and out, quickly. A python testing its food.

I hate this kind of thing. Who do they think they are, these men? I've had my fill of it. I give him the finger, slowly and deliberately. He picked the wrong day to mess with me, I think to myself. I take a sip of coffee.

He's still there.

I glance over briefly and he's making the gesture with his tongue again. I can't believe this. He's from the convenience store, I realize. He has on a fishing hat with lures stuck in it. I saw him back there, but I can't remember if he was sitting with the other men or by himself. He's big, overweight, and dirty, wearing a thin unbuttoned shirt and the terrible fishing hat. His passenger-side window is down. He begins screaming at me.

He followed me from that convenience store. The road is endless, in front there is nothing, no cars, no anything, behind is the same. Just road and grass and trees. The other two lanes are still invisible behind their screen of trees. I'm all alone out here. With him. He's screaming and screaming at me, reaching out his right arm like he's throttling me. I speed up. He speeds up, too, next to me. We're only a few feet apart, my window won't roll up.

He's got slobber on his face and there's no one in either direction. I slam on my brakes and for an instant he's ahead of me, I can breathe, then he slams on his brakes and we're next to each other again. I can't even repeat what he's screaming at me. He's telling me, amid the hot wind and poor Neil Young, what he wants to do to me. He wants to kill me. He's screaming and screaming, I can't look over.

I stare straight ahead through the windshield, hands at ten and two. The front end of his car is moving into my lane. He's saying he'll cut me with a knife, how he'll do it, all that. I can't listen. The front end of his Impala is about four inches from my white Mazda, my little car. This is really my husband's car, my beloved's. My Volkswagen died a lingering death a few months ago. There is no husband, there is no Volkswagen, there is nothing. There isn't even a Jo Ann right now. Whatever I am is sitting here clenched, hands on the wheel, I've stopped being her, now I'm something else. I'm absolutely terrified. He won't stop screaming it, over and over, what he's going to do.

I refuse to give him an inch. I will not move one inch over. If I do he'll have me off the road in an instant. I will not move. I speed up, he speeds up, I slow down, he slows down, I can see him out of the corner of my eye, driving with one hand, reaching like he's grabbing me with the other. "You whore," he screams at me. "I'll *kill* you, I'll *kill* you, I'll *kill* you . . . "

He'll kill me.

If I give him an inch, he'll shove me off the road and get his hands on me, then the end will begin in some unimaginable, unspeakable style that will be all his. I'll be an actor in his drama. We're going too fast, I've got the pedal pressed up to 80 and it's wobbling, his old Impala can probably go 140 on a straightaway like this. There will be blood, he won't want me to die quickly.

I will not lose control, I will ride it out, I cannot let him push me over onto the gravel. His car noses less than two inches from mine; I'm getting rattled. My God, he can almost reach me through his window, he's moved over in his seat, driving just with the left hand, the right is grabbing the hot air. I move over to the edge of my seat, toward the center of the car, carefully, without swerving.

In the rearview mirror a speck appears. Don't look, watch your front end. I glance up again; it's a truck. He can't get me. It's a trucker. Without looking at him I jerk my thumb backward to show him. He screams and screams and screams. He's not leaving. Suddenly a road appears on the right, a dirty and rutted thing leading off into the trees. He hits the brakes, drops behind, and takes it. In my rearview mirror I see that the license plate on the front of his car is buried in dried mud. That road is where he was hoping to push me. He wanted to push my car off the highway and get me on that road. He was hoping to kill me. He was hoping to do what maniacs, furious men, do to women alongside roads, in woods. I can't stop pressing too hard on the gas pedal. I'm at 85 now, and my leg is shaking uncontrollably, coffee is spilled all over the passenger seat, the atlas is wet, Neil Young is still howling on the tape deck. By force of will, I slow down to 65, eject the tape, and wait for the truck to overtake me. When it does, when it comes up alongside me, I don't look over at all, I keep my eyes straight ahead. As it moves in front of me I speed up enough to stay two car lengths behind it. It says *England* on the back, ornate red letters outlined in black. England.

That guy chased me on purpose, he *hated* me, with more passion than anyone has ever felt for me. Ever. Out there are all those decomposing bodies, all those disappeared daughters, discovered by joggers and hunters, their bodies long abandoned, the memory of final desperate moments lingering on the leaves, the trees, the mindless stumps and mushrooms. Images taped to tollbooth windows, faces pressed into the dirt alongside a path somewhere.

I want out of Alabama, I want to be in England. The air is still a blast furnace. I want to roll my window up, but I'd have to stop and get the crank out and lift it by hand. I'm too scared. He's out there still, waiting behind the screen of trees. I have to follow England until I'm out of Alabama. Green car, old Impala, unreadable license plate, lots of rust. Seat covers made out of that spongy stuff, something standing on the dashboard, a coffee cup or a sad Jesus. The fishing hat with a sweat ring around it right above the brim. Lures with feathers and barbs. I've never been so close to so much hatred in my whole life. *He wanted to kill me.* Think of England, with its white cows and broken-toothed farmers and dark green pastures. Think of the Beatles. I'm hugging the truck so closely now I'm almost under it. Me, of all people, he wanted to kill. Me.

Everywhere I go I'm finding out new things about myself. Each way I turn, there it is. It's Jo Ann he wanted to kill.

By noon I want to kill him. I took a right somewhere and got onto the interstate, had the nerve to pee in a rest area, adrenaline running like an engine inside me, my keys threaded through my fingers in case anyone tried anything. I didn't do anything to earn it, I realize. His anger. I didn't do anything. Unless you count giving him the finger, which I don't. *He* earned that.

As it turned out, my husband couldn't bring himself to leave me when I got back to Iowa, so I waited awhile, and watched, then disentangled myself. History: We each got ten photo albums and six trays of slides. We took a lot of pictures in thirteen years. In the early years he looks stoned and contented, distant; in the later years he looks straight and slightly worried. In that last year he only appears by chance, near the edges, a blur of suffering, almost out of frame.

Just before we split, when we were driving somewhere, I told him about the guy in the green car. "Wow," he said. Then he turned up the radio, checked his image in the rearview mirror, and smiled sincerely at the passing landscape.

The Boys of My Youth

*W*e adore *Dave Anderson. He plays* basketball in his driveway for hours each day, dribble, fake-out, shoot, dribble some more. He has smooth brown hair cut straight across his forehead, like the Dave Clark Five Dave. We watch him until we're so bored we're falling asleep, then we call him up. It's like a commercial during a TV show. His mom hollers at him, he sets the ball down, steadies it with his foot, opens the screen door, and gives it a kick back against the house so it shuts with a flat slam. The last thing we see is tennis-shoe rubber. We always hang up after he says hello, and then a minute later he's back out, drinking a bottle of Pepsi that he holds by the neck, walking around the court, dribbling in slow motion. He has no idea it's us.

We're not even boy-crazy, just bored, watching him from Elizabeth's bedroom window. She has antiqued French Provincial furniture and a princess telephone. The room is a converted front porch, with floor-to-ceiling windows and a barricaded door we use as an escape hatch on summer nights.

We're reclining on the canopied bed, Elizabeth holding back the curtains with her toes so we can watch him without sitting up. We're getting ready to dial him again, although we just did this less than an hour ago.

"She won't call him in," I predict. Dave's mother has a good sense of humor but it's wearing thin.

"This time I'm telling her who it is," Elizabeth says, dialing with a pencil. There's a chance she'll panic and hand the phone to me so I roll off the bed and stand up for a while, out of range. I have my hair in two pigtails, thin ones, and I try to fluff them up a little bit.

"You just wrecked them," Elizabeth informs me, and then suddenly looks alert. "Hello? Is Dave there?" A moment of silence while she listens. "Could you just tell him it's Brenda?" Brenda is the name of the most popular ninth-grader. We're seventh-graders. Brenda wouldn't be caught dead doing what we're doing.

"She's getting him!" Elizabeth freaks out, tries to force the phone on me. I won't take it and the receiver lies on the bed while we gesture to each other silently. Finally I hold it and we both listen, breathing steadily while he says his Hello? Hello? Just when we think he's getting ready to hang up he says, in a controlled ninth-grader voice, "*I know who this is.*"

I jam the receiver back on its cradle and we go nuts, leaping off the bed and running into each other. We pull the curtains shut and overlap them, Elizabeth gets a bobby pin from her dresser and pins them shut. We sit on the floor panting and staring at each other, wild-eyed and no longer bored.

———

My best friend Elizabeth is tall, with lanky blond hair that looks like straw, a long thin face, and black-rimmed glasses in front of green eyes. These are her pre-beautiful days. I'm short and skinny with a pale face and limp brown hair. People are always asking me if I feel well.

We met in French class, taught by Mrs. McLaughlin, the wife of Mr. McLaughlin, who teaches civics. She's the cheerleading coach, if that gives you any idea, snake-thin with a lantern jaw and hair teased into a brown bubble. She's a monster, although her husband is likable enough.

We all had to take French names, chosen from a list that got passed around the first day. We sat in alphabetical order and my last name starts with a *B* so I got a good one: Colette. Elizabeth, unfortunately, ended up with Georgette, because she comes at the end of the alphabet. In retrospect, I kind of like the name Georgette, but at the time it was the kiss of death. It sounds like the parents were hoping for a boy.

First week of junior high, everyone is terrified of their lockers and the hall monitors. It's the year of the tent dress and loud prints, so all the girls look like small hot-air balloons. Fishnet stockings are not allowed, and dresses can be no shorter than two inches above the knee. People are getting busted left and right for that one, sent to the main office where they have to kneel next to a yardstick. If your dress is too short you get sent home, no discussion.

"What if you just happen to *grow?*" Betsy Thomason asks hotly as she's sent from the room by Mrs. McLaughlin.

"I'd suggest you not," Mrs. McLaughlin replies lightly. She rolls her eyes at us in a conspiratorial way, says something in French, and we all titter uncertainly. She's wearing a pale green mohair suit, cinnamon hose, and dark green lizard skin high heels. She weighs about ninety-eight pounds, smells like cigarette smoke, her lipstick goes up above her top lip an eighth of an inch. The cheerleaders sit on her desk before class starts and trade jokes with her; they call her Mrs. Mick. Everyone else is utterly terrified of her. Suddenly she stops horsing around and looks directly at me, Colette.

"*Ou est la bibliothèque?*" she asks. I stare at her blankly, with a roaring in my ears. I'm so thin my nylons collect in pools at the knees and ankles, I'm wearing a pink plaid dress made out of spongy material, my hair is shoulder-length and supposedly curled into a flip. It's so fine that my ears stick out on either side of my head. Everyone is turned toward me.

I tilt my head to the side and pretend I can almost think of it. The roaring is louder, like seashells are clamped to my head, my heart is clattering. *Ou est la bibliothèque* . . . I've heard that somewhere before. Chances are it was last night, listening to my French dialogue record.

"Colette?" she says. "*Ou est la bibliothèque, s'il vous plait?*"

Now, *s'il vous plait* I've heard of. It means either please or thank you. I somehow manage to disengage myself, and join the other students and Mrs. McLaughlin as they stare at poor Colette, who is thinking with her head tipped to the side, her hair resting on her shoulders in horizontal sausages.

Mrs. McLaughlin finally makes a French-sounding noise of disgust and moves on. As her eyes scan the crowd, I enter my body again, and tug on my dress. She fixes her pewter gaze on the girl sitting in the last seat in the last row. This girl has straw-colored hair falling forward and bangs that come straight down and then swerve to the right. She is looking at the wall next to her intently.

"Georgette?" Mrs. McLaughlin says. "*Ou est la bibliothèque?*" Georgette continues to watch the wall, but her left cheek, the visible one, slowly turns red beneath its curtain of hair. Seconds tick past and then she whispers something.

"*Pardon*, Georgette?" Mrs. McLaughlin moves down the aisle to get a better view.

"*Près d'ici,*" Georgette says softly. Then a little louder, "*Près d'ici.*"

"If you were in France, no one would be able to understand you," Mrs. McLaughlin says shortly. "Take your hand away from your mouth and roll your *r.*" She waits.

"Okay," Georgette says desperately; she holds her hands away from her mouth but they hover in the air about six inches above her desk. "Okay, *pway dee-cee.*"

Mrs. McLaughlin lets out a genuine laugh, for an instant you can see how Mr. McLaughlin might have ended up marrying her. Then her eyes crinkle at the corners and she exclaims meanly, "You sound like Porky the Pig!" She laughs again, and then says, "*Pway d'ici,*" in a sputtering fat-cheeked way.

Georgette allows her hands to come back up to her face. She pushes her glasses up and stares once again intently at the wall. The minute hand crawls around the face of the clock, others are called on, dialogue is read out of the book, words are written on the board. At some point I look over at Georgette just as she looks at me. I shake my head, almost imperceptibly, in disbelief; she widens her eyes for an instant, mimicking a look of abject terror.

"That was ninth grade, not seventh," Elizabeth says. "We were already friends when that happened." She's at her office in downtown Chicago, talking to me on the WATS line. "You wouldn't believe what my desk looks like right now."

I would because I've witnessed it. She's an editor, and there are manuscripts stacked everywhere and yellow notes with *Urgent* scrawled across them stuck to the carpet. Her office is a wall that's a window surrounded by three orange head-high partitions. The view is of Lake Michigan, and at least in the summer it's spectacular, white triangles of boat sails and a stretching blue horizon. Thumbtacked to the partition next to her desk is a photograph of her and me at age twelve, wearing matching lime green shorts (stretchy) and dark green men's T-shirts (baggy). We both have our hair in braids, mine as slim as snakes, hers thick and bushy. We've got variegated green yarn tied in bows at the ends. We're draped across her canopy bed, listening to records and enjoying our outfits.

"They're actually making me work," she says disconsolately. I can hear her rifling through papers. I'm at work, too, and I'm an editor, too. My office is in a small town in Iowa, and it's neat and tidy in a very annoying way, according to my co-workers. There's a picture on my bulletin board of the two of us when we were in love with Dave Anderson. We are lying backward against the sloping front terrace of her yard, we have on light blue shorts (stretchy) and dark blue men's T-shirts (baggy); we're using our bodies to form the letter D. I pass this tidbit along to Elizabeth.

"He must've thought we were nuts," she replies. "What did we have on?"

I tell her. "Did we shoplift those shorts?" she asks.

We never shoplifted anything; we were too scared. "I think I did, didn't I?" she says uncertainly. "Like underpants or something, and you were chicken?" That rings a bell with me, but I can't quite place it. So, if we didn't meet in French class, then how did we meet?

She thinks for a minute. "I have no idea," she says. "We just *met*, that's how we met." More paper rifling. "I'll try to remember and then call you after lunch. I have to proofread this thing this afternoon." She can proof a manuscript and talk on the phone at the same time; so can I. In school, we had a policy of never studying unless it was absolutely necessary, and still got high-to-mediocre grades. This convinced us that we were smarter than the average citizen, and actually, we're still thinking that way. It might be one of the reasons our husbands divorced us.

We're in our late thirties, childless, and were flung at the same time out of our marriages and back into teenagehood. We spend an hour on the telephone each week talking about boys and clothes. We alternate between hating our exes in a robust, vociferous style, and lying paralyzed on our living room floors sobbing.

"Of *course* you're lying on the floor," I tell her consolingly. It's a Tuesday morning and I'm ready to leave for work. She just called me from her house in Chicago; she's in her underwear, stretched out full length alongside her coffee table. She's just realized that the husband who recently left her really *did* recently leave her. "I didn't believe it was actually happening," she says into the receiver. She's completely stuffed up and having an asthma attack at the same time. I can hear her spraying her inhaler every few minutes. Talking about her divorce is making me think of my own, and I feel like I suddenly need my inhaler, too. I set the phone down quietly while she's weeping and run into the bathroom to retrieve it.

"I'm having an asthma attack," I tell her.

"Welcome to the *club*," she replies. "The *divorce* club." She's coming out of it a little.

"Can you get up yet?" I ask her. She thinks maybe she can, so I direct her into her bedroom where she starts going through the clothes in her closet. She's on the cordless phone and we have to talk around a big annoying hiss in the background. She picks out something to wear and gets dressed, putting the phone down once to pull a shirt over her head. I keep taking short, recreational hits from my inhaler as I talk her through it. Faint voices distinguish themselves inside the phone hiss, the content is blurred but emotion comes through. The voices rise and fall.

"Who *are* those people?" she asks once, cheerfully. The crisis has passed.

Fall of our eighth-grade year, her sister-in-law has come to stay with them for a while. She's from Thailand, her name is Jinn, and she has a flat, beautiful face and black hair that reaches to her waist in long oily ropes. She is nine months pregnant and perpetually drowsy, alternating her time between sleeping on the living room couch, watching television, and cooking outlandish food that no one else will touch. She eats sitting at the kitchen table with her eyes closed, wielding chopsticks expertly and humming a song called "Kowloon Hong Kong" that she plays over and over on the hi-fi. The woman on the record jacket looks like Jinn, with a large paper flower behind one ear and black hair wound up and held in place with pointy sticks. Her voice is high and lilting, and basically off-key. We know all the words, even though they aren't in our language. I'm not sure what Jinn is doing here, I've never asked. Elizabeth's stepbrother is in the service, and stares out at everyone from a lacy metal frame on top of the television. He's round-faced and wears a white hat and a navy blue coat with ribbons on the lapel. His cheeks are pink and airbrushed and the whites of his eyes have been enhanced. If the baby turns out to be a boy it will be named Hugh, after him; if it's a girl it will be named Angelique, after a character on *Dark Shadows,* which we all watch religiously each afternoon at three. It comes on right before *The Addams Family,* a show that Jinn dismisses with a grunt and a wave of the hand before turning over on the couch and returning to an unconscious state. She speaks English just fine, but it hardly ever occurs to us to talk to her. We treat her like one of the cats, minus the torture. We ignore her unless she can do us a favor.

Sunday afternoon, family cookout at Blackhawk State Park, Elizabeth and I spend our time looking for boys and trying to act like we're not with her parents. Jinn sits at the picnic table reading a magazine from Thailand full of hieroglyphics and cigarette advertisements. Elizabeth's stepfather turns pieces of chicken on the grill. He has a friendly disposition, warm brown eyes, and a slight limp left over from a stroke. Elizabeth's mother is a little less personable, as are all our friends' mothers. Everyone I know has a mother who operates on the fringes of what's appropriate. Elizabeth's mother, Doris, was especially excitable, and relied on us to calm her down.

"Shut up, Mother," Elizabeth would tell her. Most of the time Doris would shut up, but occasionally it struck her the wrong way and all manner of hell would break loose. One time she chased Elizabeth into the bathtub and then threw a pop bottle at her. It broke and glass went everywhere except on Elizabeth, who nevertheless screamed bloody murder and threatened to call the police. I snuck home during that one, and Jinn put a pillow over her head. Afterward Doris took to her bed with a bad back and had to be waited on for a week. Elizabeth was supposedly grounded, which, in practice, meant she wasn't.

So, the picnic. Elizabeth and I entertain ourselves by putting Styrofoam cups on the ends of sticks and holding them like marshmallows over the burning coals. They melt and run fantastically, forming odd arty-looking shapes that impress us. We give each one a name and make plans to spray-paint them when we get home. A rowboat full of boys goes by out in the water and we find a reason to wander down there, where we look upriver and downriver but see no other likely suspects. Suddenly we are being summoned, and quickly, from the picnic area. We head back up at an obedient trot and discover that Jinn has gone into labor sometime after the meal. She didn't say anything, but stopped reading her magazine and began hold-

ing her stomach. Pretty soon she was groaning, a big splash occurred, and then everyone was in a hurry.

They made us put our art-cups in the trunk along with all
the other crammed-in picnic stuff. Jinn sat in the front seat between Elizabeth's parents, and Elizabeth and I had the back
seat to ourselves. Her father actually laid rubber leaving the
parking lot but then settled down and drove responsibly
through the streets of our city. Most of the way Jinn was silent
but every once in a while she would gasp out a long word in
Thai that sounded like swearing because it started with an *f*.

None of us were trying to comfort her. Elizabeth and I were
slightly out of control, hanging our heads out the car windows
and silently screaming *We're having a baby!* to each other.
Her dad said, in a cheerful voice, "Make way, we're coming
through," every time a stoplight appeared up ahead, while her
mom kept murmuring, "How are we doing," and casting side-
long glances at Jinn, who had her eyes closed and was saying
the Thai swear word quietly over and over. Suddenly she made
an *oof* noise, like someone had punched her, and then pro-
duced a muffled scream. Doris glanced at us in the back seat,
where we had quieted down and were coming to the mutual,
silent conclusion that we'd never have children.

Jinn screamed again, a short burst, and Elizabeth said, "*Mom*,"
two syllables, in an accusing voice.

"*We're doing the best we can do*," Doris said in a defensive
voice. You could tell she thought this was all her fault, and that
Elizabeth agreed. I stared out my car window and watched
houses going by at a steady clip, refusing to let the sound coming from Jinn get from my ears to my brain. Soon enough we
were at the door of the emergency room, and the two females
in the front seat got out and went in, Jinn with one hand on
her back and one clamped to her mouth, Doris looking frazzled
and unprepared.

I got dropped off at my house and Elizabeth and her stepdad went home to theirs.

"Well, I just saw somebody having a *baby*," I reported to my mother. "Right at the *picnic*." She finds this news highly interesting but I don't have much more to say. My older sister follows me upstairs and I tell her everything. "The entire back of her dress was *soaked*," I say. I shudder. "She was in agony, *screaming*, but don't tell Mom." Our mother isn't keen on extremes of any sort, or on foreigners. For that matter, she doesn't care much for Elizabeth's family, because she thinks they're different from us. The only difference I can see is that the dad isn't an alcoholic, but I don't mention that to her. She's known for getting in bad moods and grounding people for no reason. In the particular case of my older sister who has a mouth on her, my mother is prone to face slaps at odd moments. My sister takes it standing up, sometimes saying "*That* didn't hurt" before stomping upstairs and throwing my clothes all over the place.

Later in the evening Elizabeth telephones. "I can't talk," she says, "because we might get a call from the hospital." Nevertheless, we spend forty minutes on a review of the afternoon, the boys in the rowboat getting as much airtime as the pregnant lady in the car.

The next morning Elizabeth shows up at the usual time to walk to school with me. I see her coming up the back walk with her head down, yellow hair covering her face. She looks mad.

I ask her if the baby got born. She pushes past me and goes into the living room, sits on the couch and presses her face into the back of it. She starts crying loudly and can't stop.

"It *died*," she says furiously, "and it was a *girl*." At this she begins afresh, with her hands over her cheeks and her mouth a grimace.

My mother is in the kitchen eating oatmeal before work, my dad is shaving using the mirror hanging on the kitchen door.

He stops whistling and takes himself upstairs, my mother comes in the living room and looks at Elizabeth.

"Oh Liz, that's awful," she says. She feels truly bad, I can tell, but she also figures it was to be expected, I can tell that too. I feel somber and useless, I've never seen Elizabeth cry like that, even after the pop-bottle-in-the-tub business. This is something only the moms can handle; mine calls hers, Elizabeth gets sent back home, and I go off to school alone, in a stupid dress that doesn't look right.

Later we talk about it between ourselves, but we don't say a word to Jinn. She goes on, shell-shocked, her beautiful face flat as a photograph and expressionless. She continues to watch *Dark Shadows* and listen to "Kowloon Hong Kong," she continues to doze at the kitchen table and on the couch, she glides through the rooms of the apartment in her flowered housecoat as she always did, as visible and invisible as one of the cats.

Eighth grade, spring, between classes. The hallway is damp and swampy, loud with clanging lockers and the clamor of overstimulation; popular kids are being hailed, unpopular ones hooted at. A drinking fountain, a line in front of it, me in an impossibly short skirt and white knee socks. The dress code has been lifted for three months now, the boys wear pants as tight as long-line girdles and the girls wear hip-hugger skirts that are less than a foot long. Getting a drink at the fountain involves a cross between kneeling and squatting. The boy in front of me suddenly steps to the side, turns on the fountain, and with a sweep of his left hand says, "After you, my dear." I die, recover, squat/kneel, drink, put my head down, and scuttle away, wiping my chin.

I have just discovered love. The *real* thing, none of this Dave Anderson crap.

In the stairwell, I notice for the first time that outside the window the ground is soaked and emerald-colored, jonquils lie supine in the rain, tulips are lolling their fat heads. I take the stairs three at a time, turning my miniskirt into a wide belt, race down the hall to Elizabeth's home-ec class and grab her as she's going in.

"Get sick," I tell her.

"We're making Rice Krispies treats," she says. "Wait 'til math."

"I *can't* wait, I'm *dy*ing," I say pleadingly, and then, because I know it's true: "*You'll* die too."

Fifteen minutes later we are reclining side by side on two narrow cots in the nurse's office. Elizabeth has a tremendous headache that requires a washcloth draped across her forehead, I have a tremendous stomachache that requires a metal bowl balanced on my chest.

I'm in love, it's serious, he's beyond what we've encountered before. He is like a *Beatle*, he's that cute. No kidding, honest to God, et cetera.

"He said 'my dear'?" she asks in a hoarse whisper. "He sounds like a queeb."

He's not a queeb, you had to be there. He made it sound *funny*. Not queebie at *all*, in fact, just the opposite. He's the opposite.

The nurse pokes her head in and we both groan. "No talking," she says.

"We weren't," we say in unison.

Elizabeth is willing to fall in love with him, too, but she needs to see him first, as a formality. We agree to meet after class at the fountain, in case he comes back for another drink. We go out and tell the nurse we're better. She sends Elizabeth back to home-ec but makes me go lie down again.

"You're still pale," she says shortly.

He doesn't show up at the drinking fountain again, but after school we go to my house to pore over last year's yearbook. I have a feeling he's older than us, and it's true. We find him among last year's eighth-graders.

"Jeff Bach," I announce, and hand the yearbook over. We're in my living room eating Fritos and drinking pop. My sister hasn't gotten home from high school yet so we're safe, nobody's bugging us.

"He's got blond hair," she remarks, staring at the picture closely. She takes another handful of Fritos. "I thought you said he looked like a Beatle." She puts them in her mouth.

"I said he's as cute *as* a Beatle," I reply. "Not that he *was* a Beatle."

She stares at his face intently as she chews, and then comes to a conclusion. "Let's face it," she proclaims, "he's *cuter* than a Beatle."

We're both in love with Jeff Bach, ninth-grader extraordinaire.

The back door slams and my sister appears in the doorway to the living room. She is wearing a granny dress, her thick brown hair tucked into a crocheted snood at the nape of her neck. She arches her brows. "How's kindergarten?" she asks. She takes the bag of Fritos from Elizabeth's lap and heads upstairs with it. "Clean this house up," she says as she rounds the curve at the landing.

We leave and walk over to Elizabeth's house, where we tell Jinn about our new boyfriend. We get Elizabeth's yearbook and make her look at the picture. "Blond," she says politely, and turns her eyes back to the television. Pretty soon Elizabeth's stepdad comes home from work. We show him the picture. "How would you like it if I married *this* guy?" Elizabeth asks him rhetorically. He says he'd like it just fine and asks why the newspaper hasn't come yet.

"Who knows, that's why," Elizabeth replies. I get killed if

I'm not there when my mother gets home from work, so I leave and call up Elizabeth ten minutes later from two blocks over.

"What're you doing?" I ask.

There are four girls in our group, plus two best friends who hang around with another group approximately half the time. Besides Elizabeth and me there are Madelyn and Renee, and the two best friends, Carol and Janet. Renee is the oldest of six kids and we stay overnight at her house a lot because both her parents work nights at the post office and leave Renee in charge. They live in a big old house with three floors, and it never seems like there is any food except long loaves of sandwich bread, giant boxes of generic cereal, and powdered milk. If you're looking for mustard, or a bottle of pop, forget it. Renee is the only kid in the family with a room of her own and she keeps potato chips and Pop-tarts in her closet, which locks with a skeleton key. Each bedroom has a fire escape ladder in a metal box underneath the window.

Madelyn is destined to move away unexpectedly when we're in ninth grade, and all I can remember about her is that she was funny and mean, and that she threw a half pound of frozen hamburger at her mother once when she was told she couldn't go to a movie.

"Plus her dad slept in a coffin," Elizabeth reminds me. She has called me from her bathtub, the water is still running and she's talking loudly to compensate. "I saw him taking a nap in it once; it was a black box without a lid, and the headboard said *R.I.P.*"

"What a sicko," I say.

"No kidding," she agrees. The sound of water running stops abruptly, a splash is heard. "Wasn't there something suspicious about him?"

"That was Renee's dad." Renee's dad made everyone un-comfortable, he was very young, just like her mom, and he talked to us like we were adults. He flirted with us, except we didn't identify it as that, because he was a dad. We took on nervous smiles and sidled backward whenever he was around.

"There was more to *that* story than met the eye," she said, then, "hang on," and the sound of a giant lapping wave comes through the phone. "Jo Ann?" she says loudly. "*Jo Ann?* I dunked my head; now I've got water in my ears."

I feel cranky suddenly, and want to get off the phone. "Don't *call* me when you're in the bathtub," I say. "I don't want to listen to your personal hygiene. And I'm late for something."

"Buh-ruther," she says sarcastically. "What did I do? I dunked my head, big deal; how'm I supposed to wash my hair?"

"How about on your own time, that ever occur to you?"

"*How about if I smack your head off?*" and she slams her phone down with a huge noise.

We are thirty-eight years old. I wait fifteen minutes and call her back.

"Hi," she says. "Guess what I got in the mail?"

Divorce papers, with a smiley face on a Post-it note from her husband. "That was bugging me, you in the bathtub," I tell her. "Jim's the one who should get his head smacked off. Or Tina." Tina is Jim's receptionist, and the woman he left Elizabeth for.

"I'm not smacking anybody's head off," she replies dreamily. "Because I don't even care." When Jim first left her for Tina, Elizabeth made the mistake of asking why, and he told her. In the course of the conversation he mentioned a specific sex act that men tend to like a lot.

"You're kidding," I said.

"Not only am I not kidding," she replied. "But the thing is, it's true. I mean, you hate to simplify these things, but he's the one who said it." She sighed hugely. "That's what they sit around doing."

Her voice had the same dreamy quality it has now, but a week later, when it had sunk in, she'd been ready to take out after him with a baseball bat. She'd tried to call him at work to tell him he was a dead man, but Tina wouldn't put her through. "Uh, I don't *think* so, Liz," she had said smugly, right before disconnecting her.

So, any idea why Madelyn's dad slept in a coffin?

"He thought it was funny, of course," she said. "Men."

Jeff Bach, blond, the fifth Beatle, a student at our school. Lived below the hill and hung around with guys who were Mexican, which made him seem even more blond. Danny Garcia, one of his friends, yanks on my hair in science.

"Hey," he whispers. "You and Liz like Jeff."

I turn around and roll my eyes, trying for sarcasm. "I'm *sure*," I whisper back.

Forty minutes later, Elizabeth and I are side by side in the nurse's office. The next cot is occupied by someone who appears to be truly sick, not faking it. The nurse is excited by this and keeps poking her head in and staring at him.

News has been leaked, if Danny Garcia knows then everyone knows. If everyone knows, then Jeff must know. We think we could actually puke; we groan and stare at the paint on the ceiling. The nurse hears us and thinks she might have an epidemic on her hands.

"You should've said *Jeff who*," Elizabeth hisses.

I never thought of that. I start pretending like I'm beating myself up. We do our silent screaming routine. The guy on the other cot opens one eye. "I'm not really sick," he says.

High School

"Us neither," we whisper back.

Pretty soon they both go back to class and I get kept for another hour and released at lunch.

"Eat some meat if you can," the nurse advises.

husband

My own husband didn't have a receptionist, but he had a best friend, and the best friend had a wife. On a bitterly cold Sunday morning he went out to get doughnuts and didn't return for two hours. I took a bath, using my toes to turn the hot water on and off. Pretty soon my knees were brilliant pink, my forehead was sweating, and it came to me that I'd been in there a while. I wondered how come my doughnuts weren't back yet and then suddenly the answer hit me, the way a math problem can solve itself when you're not paying attention. *Oh*, I thought, *he's having an affair.* I stood up immediately, like the tub had ejected me, and began drying off.

When he came home I was dressed, standing in the middle of the living room with an ashtray in my hand, smoking a stale French cigarette I'd found in my desk. I hadn't smoked for four years but was quickly getting the hang of it again; only halfway through my first cigarette, and I already wanted another one. He was clattering around in the kitchen, putting breakfast on a blue plate, pouring a cup of coffee. I prepared a smoke ring and launched it in his direction as he walked into the living room.

He stopped. "What?" he said. His face turned into clay; on the blue plate were giant melting doughnuts, some with multicolored dots on top, some with white cream oozing from their back ends. "What?" he said again.

I told him and he didn't disagree. The only thing that happened was his face twitched, like a horse's hide, when I said the word. *Affair.* You are. And I am very. Upset. Actually I also wailed, like a baby in its crib. That scared him and he set down the doughnuts and coffee, took a step toward me, a step back, then sat down on the edge of the couch. Unbelievably, he began to cry, which shut me up instantly.

Do I want to know who?

This from my husband Eric, who had held my hand when they lowered my mother into the ground, who put me in a bathtub once and poured cold water on me to break a fever, who whispered the names of the constellations again and again because I could never remember them. I guess I need to know who.

He tells me the name and the howling baby comes out again before I collect myself. *Kim?* She's a passive-aggressive *rat*, everyone knows that, *nobody* likes her. You like *her?*

Not really, he acknowledges. In some ways she's pathetic, the way she lets Bruce talk to her. He's no longer crying, he suddenly looks pious and overburdened. In as flat a voice as I can manage I suggest he go sit around somebody else's house for a while.

When the door closes behind him I stand in the center of the room and light another prehistoric cigarette. Off in the distance the phone rings. It's Bruce, wondering if Eric's around. I set the receiver back in the cradle without saying a word, and as I do so, the house settles over my shoulders like a stucco cape.

A spring night, one A.M., we have just escaped through the barricaded door of Elizabeth's bedroom into the inky darkness. We let our eyes adjust, breathing in the dusty smell of geraniums. A bridal wreath bush stands laden with tiny white bouquets, the sky is velvety beyond the branches of a sycamore, the stars are tiny pinpricks of light. We have six half-rolls of toilet paper borrowed from various gas stations and public toilets. We are on a mission.

"Let's go," I whisper and we move out silently, going from house to house, staying in the black shadows of the flowering bushes. Four blocks from her house we find ourselves trapped up against a garage while a man and a woman have an argument in the driveway. They've just pulled in and gotten out of the car, a station wagon with wood on the sides. The concrete driveway is ghostly blue in the moonlight, their faces are doughy.

"Why her?" the woman says over and over again. "Why her?"

The man tries to pet her head like she's a dog. "Honey, don't," he says each time she asks why her. *Honey, don't, honey, don't, honey, don't.* And then they kiss, staggering sideways. We seem to be standing in some unflowering rose bushes, absolutely still in the darkness, like a black and white photograph of two girls who have done this before. Something hits my arm and buzzes, I look down and see a June bug flapping around. Another one hits my cheek. I take Elizabeth's elbow and try to pull her away. She resists and glares at me, points one finger toward the people standing in a blue pool of moonlight twenty feet away. I grab her arm and yank her onto the driveway and run through the next yard and the next, her panting fast and loud behind me. We're laughing silently and hysterically. A ravine appears on the right and we run for it, diving down the hill, where we lay, gasping.

"You *queeb*," Elizabeth whispers. She punches me in the arm. "Why did you *do* that?"

I pause. "There were June bugs smacking into me," I tell her gently.

She immediately stops laughing and squeezes her eyes shut. A moan escapes from her lips. "I can't," she says without opening her eyes. "I can't keep going if there are June bugs."

"There aren't," I say. "It's not even June — those two are the only ones."

She still has her eyes closed. "No sir," she says in a small voice.

I try to think for a minute. Finally I say, "Don't wreck everything because of two June bugs."

She opens one eye and looks at me with it. "What about if there were *worms*, you wouldn't even walk in case one might *touch* you." I consider this a low blow and remain silent. "And you know it," she finishes.

A minute goes by, both of us staring through the ravine trees at the black sky. "You *know* it," she says once more. We get up slowly, like old people, readjust the toilet paper rolls that are tied around our waists on pieces of rope, and set out, subdued, to complete our mission.

A woman friend stops over to visit me one afternoon. She is lonely, melancholy, and at loose ends. Do you ever feel like this? she asks me. That's how the entire world feels, I say. Sit down, have some chips, have some dip. She's not one of my favorite people, but I'd rather talk to her than write, which is what I was doing when she dropped by. She's having husband troubles apparently, and winds up telling me she's thinking of having an affair.

"Have you ever done that?" she asks. Her head is tilted to the side quizzically, a trace of sour cream is adhered to her lower lip. I feel immensely warm and slightly guilty all of a sudden, and the walls of the room step in an inch or so, crowding me.

"Oh, Kim, it's not good to do that," I tell her. And I mention some lovely traits her husband Bruce has, not the least of which is that he's my own husband's best friend. She takes that for what it's worth and drifts back through the front door, gets in her little yellow car, and peels out.

———————

Danny Garcia's house is on a cul-de-sac it takes us forever to find. By this time we are walking in the no-June-bug zone in the middle of the street, and talking in normal voices. As it turns out, his house has no trees, so we're momentarily at a loss. There are small bikes and wrecked toys in the front yard, and a sign that says *Koolade 4 Sale*. We caucus for a minute, crouched next to a blue sedan parked at the curb.

"Now what are we supposed to do?" I say. Elizabeth stares up at the split-level ranch house and thinks. She outlines a plan that involves only what we have available — if there are no trees, there are no trees. Simple, really.

Twenty minutes later we have draped giant strands of toilet paper over the roof of the house, seven of them, from one end to the other. We had to hurl them, unraveling whitely against the night sky, one of us in the backyard and one in the front. Our contingency plan was if a light came on or if anyone came out, we would run in two separate directions and meet at Renee's house, five blocks away. The strands are anchored on either side of the house with trikes and dump trucks. We meet in the shadow of the blue car to survey the situation.

"It needs more," I whisper.

"I'm too tired," she whispers back.

"We walked all the way over here and it only looks like about two *strands*," I insist. "Let's just get rid of the rolls." So we patiently unwind them, leaving pools of white against the pavement. We travel back up into the yard and, carefully holding the ends, throw the rolls over the roof, one after the other. The last two don't make it, our arms are too tired, and they land with a thud and roll back down the roof and into the bushes in front of the porch. In an instant a light goes on, the door bursts open, and Danny and Stuart Garcia are running barefoot, sixty-five miles an hour. Elizabeth and I are half a block away by this time, and we veer off suddenly, one to the left, one to the right, like a dividing amoeba.

The yards are hard to navigate, there are things lying around everywhere, lawn mowers, rakes, bicycles, and, in one case, a tied-up dog who runs out to the end of his chain and stands up on his back legs, wagging his tail and pedaling his front paws. I can't tell which Garcia followed me, but I can hear him crashing around, one yard over. I stop and crouch under the awning of the dog's plywood house. The dog climbs in beside me happily and we both sit in the straw, me listening for the sounds of a Garcia, him biting a flea. There is a pale light burning in the kitchen of the house, illuminating an ornate clock and the corner of a fridge, harvest gold. Pots of African violets, a mound of spilled potting soil and a pair of gloves are sitting on a table by the back door. The dog, a beagle mix with long silky ears, leans up against me and yawns. I put one arm around him and we're buddies together, in the shade of his little abode. You can tell he doesn't get many visitors in here, but he's a good host. A gnawed-on bone is tucked in the corner. I hold it out and he tilts his head quizzically, then takes it only when he's sure I don't want it, and begins absentmindedly chewing.

From inside the plywood shelter we watch the night tick along. After fifteen minutes or so I hear voices, and I pull my legs farther inside and scrunch up into the black corner. Through the yard amble Danny and Stuart, wincing on their bare feet, talking in whispers and making little aggressive gestures toward imaginary enemies. The dog fades out into the night and stands on his hind legs again at the end of his chain. Stuart stops for a second and lets the dog rest his front paws against him. All I can see are their legs and hands, they can't see anything of me. Stuart lifts the dog's ear and touches the soft part inside. The dog stops wagging and holds himself very still, in paralyzed pleasure. They walk on, whispering, and the dog gets a drink of water from a dishpan and then wanders back into his shelter. I'm sorry, but I have to go. He's pretty philosophical about it, following me to the end of his chain and then stretching out on the damp ground, back legs stuck out terrier-style, tail moving slowly back and forth.

I walk through backyards until I get to Renee's block and then I walk in the street. One time Elizabeth, Madelyn, and I walked around this block with our shirts off and tied around our waists. It was about three in the morning and the houses were dead and silent, the streetlights shone yellow spots on the pavement. We walked and walked, with our arms over our heads, letting the night air get on our skin. I'm not in the mood for any of that nonsense tonight. There she is, sitting on Renee's front porch.

"I thought they got you," Elizabeth whispers hoarsely. Her hair is going eight different ways and her cheeks are pink, her voice is croaky.

"I went in a doghouse with a dog," I say. "And they came right past me, and are they pissed." I tell her some of the words Danny and Stuart were whispering.

"Eek," she says.

Since there are no parents on the premises, we decide to wake Renee up and tell her what happened. Through the front window we can see the two littlest kids asleep on the floor in front of the snowy TV screen. Stacy has on a diaper and socks and has her head resting on a bed pillow without a case. Amy has on a T-shirt and no pants whatsoever, and has her head resting on a skanky stuffed dinosaur. Renee is asleep on the couch under an afghan, a book open across her chest. We tap on the window. Stacy stirs and puts a thumb in her mouth. Amy rolls over so her face is against the dinosaur's face.

"Seems like a shame to wake them up," I say, and then tap louder. Renee startles awake and the book falls off her chest.

"Don't wake the babies," she whispers as she lets us in. She has drool on her from sleeping on the couch, and we don't want to point it out but we do anyway. "Oh," she says, wiping it off. We follow her out to the kitchen where she sits at the table, yawning. I sit on the counter and Elizabeth looks in the refrigerator.

"We would have been dead if they'd caught us," I tell Elizabeth. She concurs. We tell Renee what happened. She confirms what we already suspected: Stuart Garcia is dangerous. And she's in a position to know — she went steady with him in grade school.

"He wanted to drop me and go with Maria Valdez," she says sleepily. "So he threw a steak knife at me and it hit a tree. He got about forty swats with the wooden paddle from the principal." I repeat for her in great detail the words I heard him saying while I was jammed into the doghouse. It was an altogether stunning display of swearing, and we can't help but be impressed. Stuart and Danny have suddenly put themselves on the map.

"Those guys will say *anything*," Elizabeth remarks. She's having a bowl of cereal, using milk that is thin and watery with a faint blue cast.

"How's that breast milk taste?" I ask her. She stares into the bowl for a second and then shrugs, takes another spoonful.

"What would you've done if they caught you?" Renee asks. In some ways Renee is the perfect friend, she's genuinely nice and asks you just exactly the questions you are prepared to answer. She is also pretty, with thin shiny hair and round brown eyes and a mouth that smiles even when she's just reading or listening to a teacher. The boys love her, too, and cluster around her, which works out well for her friends, who are neither nice nor friendly.

"I would've just started screaming," Elizabeth answers. And it's true, we all know it.

good descript.

I make a slow-motion kicking gesture with my foot. "Right in the old codpiece," I say. Elizabeth makes a snorting noise and then has a nose attack right in Renee's kitchen. It's when she can't breathe through her mouth — she's still eating cereal — and her nostrils slam shut. She has to reach up and pry them open manually so she can get air.

I try to help her and we wake the babies up accidentally.

"Shit-fuck," Renee says wearily. The babies wander out to the kitchen, blinking their eyes in the brightness and whimpering. They both try to climb on Renee, who stares patiently at the ceiling for a second and then helps them up on her lap. They look at Elizabeth and me with blank, defensive eyes, Amy with her thumb jammed in her mouth, Stacy with her hand down her diaper.

"Do you have to go on the big-girl potty?" Renee asks her. She shakes her head no and closes her eyes. Suddenly we're all tired, even Elizabeth and me. We take the kids and Renee leads the way upstairs. She pokes her head in all the bedrooms: B.J. is asleep on Renee's bed, Alex is asleep on the rug beside his bed, Cindy is sleeping in B.J.'s bed. I have Amy, who's as heavy as a sandbag and smells like sour milk and baby shampoo. We finally put them on the king-size bed in the parents' room. There's no sheet so we cover them with the funky, crumpled-up bedspread and tiptoe out. B.J. is seven and weighs a ton so I take his feet and Elizabeth takes his arms and we carry him like a hammock between us and dump him into Cindy's bed so Renee can sleep alone. She whispers good night and we're gone, back into the cold spring air.

It takes about two blocks of freezing cold before we decide we have to ride instead of walk. We find a boy's bicycle with a long banana seat in somebody's backyard and take it; Elizabeth pedals standing up and I ride on back, with my legs stuck straight out on either side. When she gets winded I take over, but I sit while I pedal, which scrunches her. I can't help it; I'm tired.

When we get to the big hill we leave the bike leaning against a tree and trudge ourselves straight up for one block and then it's two blocks of flat ground, and then we're at her house, sneaking back in.

I go first in case somebody's up; at least we know they won't throw a pop bottle at me. The coast is clear. Elizabeth steps into her bedroom and suddenly we're wide awake again. We debate about calling up the Garcias, and then, in an unusual display of restraint, don't. Instead, we go out to the kitchen and prepare a cake mix we find in the cupboard. We take it back into the bedroom and lie on the bed in the dark, eating cherry chip cake batter with big wooden spoons. We're wound up now, it's impossible to think about sleeping.

We discuss the Jeff Bach situation for a while. We come to the conclusion that it's hard to like someone so blond. "I like dark-haired guys, I think," Elizabeth says. I can see the shadow of her profile in the bed, she's gesturing with her wooden spoon.

"Me too," I say.

There is a long silence. It's late, four A.M. or something. We're finally getting tired again. She puts the batter on the floor next to the bed; I hand her my spoon and she drops it into the bowl. A few minutes pass.

"I might like Danny Garcia," she says tentatively. Another minute goes by.

"I might like Stuart," I say. She thinks this over. I turn on my side and she cuddles up right behind me; we sleep like two spoons whenever we're in the same bed.

"Stuart's dangerous," she whispers.

"I know it," I say softly, into the darkness, and then we're both asleep.

It's nineteen seventy-something, summer, nighttime, black country road running through rural Illinois, the sky is immense. Three miles ahead are train tracks that can be sailed over if you approach them right, all four tires will leave the ground at once. We're heading for our house, a two-story farm job with a big garden out back, a bunch of pigs that are not our responsibility, a summer kitchen with spiders and mice, and two dogs who wait patiently all day for us to get home so their lives can begin. I've thrown my lot in with the guy in the driver's seat, and he with me. We're both certain we'll never amount to anything, which only bothers us when we think about it. Right now we're high on dope and each other, and the night air smells like rain. The road is white where the headlights hit it, and everything else is pure black. The car is old and bumperless, with a plywood fender that has a dent where an agitated friend of ours karate-chopped it. The tape deck is not for the faint-hearted; the sound inside the car is huge and all-consuming. Right now it sounds like someone is playing a guitar using a razor blade for a pick, and the question being asked is Are you experienced? The answer is No, we aren't, but we're working on it.

Coming up on the long stretch before the giant Dip in Pavement and the subsequent railroad tracks, Eric glances over at me for an instant, assessing my mood, then pushes the lights off and we streak through the blackness down the center of the highway, dark moving inside of dark, our faces faint in the dashboard light. It sounds for a moment like the guitar player is saying Areyouanidiot? and then I decide to be into it.

I put one arm out my window, to feel the night air and create some drag. He presses harder on the gas. The sky is distinguishable from the ground only because it is blue-black, and the land is black-black. There are stars. This is what they mean by barreling down the road. Not only could this be certain death, but we may take somebody else out, too, which is troubling. He isn't thinking of any of that; in fact, he's got his eyes closed, or else just the one I can see — he's trying to freak me out. That settles it. I put my foot on top of his and press it to the floor. I close my own eyes and imagine myself leaning into it, certain death. Darkness and his girlfriend, Darkness, are out for a ride through the countryside in the summer night. We hit the dip and are airborne for a breathless millisecond, then there's that long, terrible dope-inspired instant that stretches out forever, where you don't know if there'll be a train on the tracks or not, whether you'll get to continue living.

This time we do.

"They clean your room and cook your meals so you can write about Stuart *Garcia?*" Elizabeth asks incredulously. She's at her job in Chicago.

"Apparently," I reply. I'm in the wilds of upstate New York, at an artist's colony, sitting in a phone booth drawing pictures and talking to her while she formats something on her computer, which keeps beeping.

"You should say he was dangerous," she suggests.

I hate it here; why did I come here? All there is to do is write.

"You always go through this," she reminds me. There is the sound of a tiny bomb exploding, a ding, and she exhales loudly. "I just crashed my whole computer," she explains.

"I just crashed my whole life," I tell her mournfully. I'm afraid she's going to try to hang up. "Who even cares about the boys of my youth? There weren't any, it was all imaginary. I'm making it up as I go along." I draw a picture of a pit bull on the phone book in the phone booth. It has pointy ears, bowed legs, and giant teeth. "Now I'm drawing a giant-toothed dog," I tell her.

"That's good," she says. "Remember that time you went to Florida to write and became troubled?"

"In the category of freak-out, *that* was the real thing." I draw a palm tree with coconuts hanging off it next to the pit bull.

"I made you eat a banana that time," she reminds me. We muse on that for a moment, until her computer comes back on line and says hello to her in a voice from outer space. We hang up.

As a matter of fact, there happens to be a banana in my lunch. Every day they give me a lunchbox with a sandwich, a piece of fruit, and a cookie in it. I eat the cookie, think about the sandwich, and put the fruit on my writing table, then I go back to staring out the window of my studio. This is how professional writers work.

I went to Florida once to work on a writing project. I borrowed a house on Key-something, with a million-mile view of the Atlantic, sliding glass doors, expensive furniture, and cockroaches the size of a man's big toe. My friend's sister, who was lending me the house, showed me how you had to spray Raid directly on the bug in order to make it die. At first it seemed unfazed, and then it wandered about a foot away and fell over. "They aren't cockroaches," she explained firmly.

"I'm not afraid of bugs," I told her. "I *like* bugs, actually." In fact, I'm married to one, is what I thought to myself. This was during a down phase in my marriage. I was there in Florida because he wouldn't stop seeing the wife of his best friend. "We're not *doing* anything," he would explain. "What are you — nuts?" The wife herself was miffed at me. "Why can't we still be friends?" she asked. I would speak to her only when cornered, and then only to call her names. She kept trying though, calling my house at odd hours to ask me how I was doing in a concerned, schoolmarmish voice.

"Quit calling my house and quit screwing my husband," I'd reply evenly. She'd sigh; I'd hang up. Once I took the phone off the wall and threw it out the front door into a snowbank. Eric retrieved it wordlessly, dried it off, hung it back on the wall. "You suck," I told him. He stared at me for a long moment and then went back to whatever he was doing.

I was trying to make him miss me by going to Florida, but it wasn't working. On the way down, while driving in my car, I would have long imaginary arguments with him, where I hit every point square on the head and he was left speechless and remorseful. I had him apologizing to me left and right, every hundred miles or so. Between that and singing to the radio, it was a pretty productive trip down.

So, my friend's sister left and I wandered around her house, upstairs, downstairs, finally setting up my typewriter in front of a large glass door that opened onto a balcony with a view of the water and some boats. I organized all my writing paraphernalia, sharpened some pencils using a paring knife from the kitchen, and then sat down and began having a nervous breakdown.

Eventually the sun dropped into the water, leaving a fakey sunset, gaudy pink and yellow stripes along the horizon. The boats disappeared, one by one, and a group of long-legged storklike birds flew past the large glass door, out over the water, and then were gone. They weren't the kind of storks that carry babies, thank God; not bothering to have a baby being one of the things I deeply regretted the minute my marriage started unraveling. As soon as it got completely dark, the glass door turned into a giant black mirror, showing a ghostly image of me sitting in a wicker chair in the dimness. My hands were folded calmly in my lap. I looked like a dark painting of barely controlled hysteria, surrounded by wicker and the long fronds of tropical plants. I felt like I was on an elevator that had burst through the top of the building and was still climbing. At some point I stood up creakily on my stiff legs and went looking for something to put me to sleep.

Three warm beers later I stretched out on the king-size bed and stared at the ceiling. I felt like myself as a six-year-old, lying in bed for hours, making up frightening stories in my head, waiting for my sister to wake up and torture me. Me as a kid: skinny and pale and jumpy, terrified of a particular cartoon character who was thin and wiry with a narrow, whiplike mustache. He wore a black outfit with a string tie and he tied girls to railroad tracks or to conveyor belts with buzz saws at the end. On the way to the bathroom, I heard the sound of a Frito crunching. It was a cockroach, stuck to my foot.

I began freaking out in earnest.

Heart pounding, I scraped the bug off, peed, and stared at myself in the dark mirror. I was spooked and looked it. I walked on my tiptoes back into the bedroom and jumped onto the bed. I pulled the sheet around me and curled into my usual sleeping position (fetal). I imagined everyone in my life abandoning me, all the while assuring me they weren't. I replayed a scene from several years ago: my mother in a hospital bed with Eric at her side, extracting a promise from him, he listening solemnly, speaking to her in a whisper, nodding, holding her hand; me in the hallway, exasperated and worn out, rolling my eyes, one last opportunity for defiance, sassing back even then.

I started a low-grade whimpering to keep myself company. It was dark and dark and dark and then it began to be light and light and then dawn showed up. I used a remote control to turn on the television and page through the channels. There was a religious program on, a Bullwinkle cartoon which was the last thing I needed, a worm's-eye view of a woman doing an aerobic workout, and CNN. I watched CNN intently, with the sound off and my eyes squinted almost shut.

I kept remembering some footage I'd seen of a plane crash that happened a few years back, where a seat with a passenger strapped to it was thrown hundreds of feet from the wreckage. The seat landed in an upright position, and the passenger, slightly charred, was sitting quietly with an arm on each armrest, deader than dead. I replayed the footage over and over, trying to make the passenger wake up, but to no avail.

At some point I went into the bathroom and threw up, then stared at myself again in the mirror, surveying the damage. My eyes looked like two red holes in a pink blanket. My stomach hurt.

I found the telephone, a cordless job, and carried it out onto the balcony with me. The Florida sun was climbing, the air felt like hot, wet lint. The same old boats were making their way back into view, chugging along silently, leaving trails of foam that leveled back out into flat blue. I sat with the phone in my hand until there was nothing left to do but dial it. I called my own number at home and a man answered. He said hello about five times and then hung up. It was my husband.

Everything was overwhelmingly bright, my eyes couldn't stand it. I went back in to the king-size bed. Suddenly the phone, still stuck to my hand, started ringing. I stared at it until it stopped. When the digital clock said 10 I called Chicago.

"Where *are* you?" Elizabeth says cheerfully. "I called you and Eric said you ran away from *home* or something."

"I'm in Florida, at Taylor's sister's house," I say. "I'm supposed to be writing."

"You sound weird," she says. "Jo Ann? You sound weird."

I am weird.

"Why are we not talking?" she asks gently. "Are we okay?"

No, unfortunately we're not. I swallow hard and stare at my clenched and hysterical feet. My stomach still hurts. I'm sitting in the center of a giant bed in a giant house on Key Nightmare.

"I'm freaking out," I tell her. "I'm ready to jump off a balcony into the sand or something."

She considers this for a long moment and then says, quietly, "Uh-oh, this is a marriage problem, right?" As far as she's concerned, her own marriage is as solid as a house, but the truth is, it's just about this time that her husband is beginning to notice what beautiful eyes his receptionist has, how the sound of her typing is like water rushing over a falls.

For about five minutes I can't talk, but instead nod or shake my head when she asks me questions. Her voice has taken on a soothing, reassuring tone I've never heard her use before. It makes me feel like crying. The bedroom is starting to really bother me so I close my eyes and grope my way out, still holding the phone to my ear.

"I'm walking," is what I finally say to her.

"*Good*," she responds quickly. "If you're walking, then you're okay."

This is encouraging, so I walk some more. I walk out onto the balcony and stare at the phony boats on the horizon. I try to tell her what is happening to me — that my heart is beating so hard my T-shirt is moving, that I threw up because of some plane crash footage I saw two years ago, that I keep remembering being stalked by a cartoon guy with a whiplike mustache and a string tie.

"Well, I hate to break it to you," she says firmly, "but that sounds like *Eric*." Eric is pretty thin and so is his mustache.

"Well, *Eric's* certainly not stalking me," I tell her. I start to cry suddenly, which is a relief. "He's doing whatever the opposite of stalking me is." Now that I'm crying I can't stop. I'm leaning over the balcony railing and tears are dropping into the sand below me. I tell Elizabeth this.

"Why don't you just *please* get off that balcony, and go back in the house?"

"I'm not going to *jump*," I say. "It's only about ten feet from the *ground*, for Chris'sakes."

"Oh," she says.

The problem is, whenever it occurs to me that he's leaving me, I start to feel like throwing up again. Also, I haven't slept for a couple of days. Or eaten. And it feels like there's an alien in my chest.

"You can't not eat," she says. "That's what we'll fix first." She sounds so confident that I feel myself relax a little. I'm still trapped in the elevator but I've lost that terrible zooming-upward vertigo feeling. I look at my feet. Under her direction, I walk downstairs with the telephone and stand in the kitchen. "Tell me everything there is to eat," she says.

One cupboard has rice cakes, spices, and vegetable oil, another has cans of things, boxes of cereal, and an envelope of mushroom soup, another has pots and pans, the refrigerator has mayonnaise and a jar of green olives. The sight of the pimientos makes me sick for a minute, I have to lean over and think of something else. When I say green olives to Elizabeth she immediately says, "Don't look at the pimientos." There is a basket in the middle of the kitchen table that holds two bananas, a paper clip, a packet of sugar substitute, a blue marble, and a ballpoint pen. "Perfect," she says.

She wants me to eat a banana.

"*Any*one can eat a banana," she says smoothly. "People give them to *babies*, they're so easy to eat."

"I'll throw up if I look at it," I tell her. My heart is pounding again.

"Oh no you won't," she tells me. "A *rice* cake would make

you throw up; bananas don't make people sick, else they wouldn't give them to babies." I can't argue with her logic, but I can't look at the bananas either. "I'm going to call you back in exactly half an hour. You take one bite every five minutes." I give her the phone number, set the telephone down on the kitchen table, and peel a banana without looking at it. Thirty minutes later the phone rings.

"I ate it," I tell her. Actually I ate half of it.

She has me take the phone in the bathroom and inventory the medicine cabinet. I do so obediently, the banana sitting in my stomach like a wad of clay. "Midol; emery board; Ramada Inn soap; Nyquil; unidentifiable pills way too big to take; sunscreen; sunscreen; eyeliner; generic aspirin; Bic razor, crusty." I sit down on the edge of the tub. The medicine cabinet has made me panicky again.

"Perfect," she says. "This is what you do now: put your swimming suit on and walk on the beach for one and a half hours, okay? Then come back and drink two doses of Nyquil and lie down on the couch. You don't have to sleep or anything, just lie down." She reiterates this. "In fact, it's actually better if you *don't* sleep." She's using reverse psychology on me.

The beach is empty, except for some old cans and a broken fishing pole. A bloated fish lies half buried in the sand, one tarnished eye staring placidly up at the sun. I step over it and make my way down the beach at the water's edge. Water is soothing, Elizabeth told me, water is soothing, water is soothing. I feel calm all of a sudden, looking at the water and the sky and the fins of sharks circling about two hundred yards out. "Those are dolphins," I say out loud. Each time I come across a bloated fish or a squashed something, I say, "That's not dead." When I feel like my legs are going to drop off I turn around and head back. By this time the sun is hanging about a quarter-inch above the part in my hair. My shoulders feel scorched and I'm sort of hungry. Back at the house I eat a rice cake with a glass of water. It tastes like Styrofoam, which is somehow better than having it taste like food. I drink as much of the Nyquil as I can stand, stretch out on the couch, and count sheep with my eyes open.

Five hours later the phone rings off in the distance and I come to. I feel swampy and disoriented, stand up quickly, and then sit back down on the couch. It's hard to tell where the phone is located. Staggering through the house, I follow the noise into the bathroom.

"Guess who," she says cheerfully. I report to her on what I've accomplished — the walk, the rice cake, the Nyquil nap. "Whew," she says. "For a minute there I thought I was gonna have to come *rescue* you; I even called the airline."

I feel deeply touched by this, and begin weeping. I'm not completely out of the woods.

"Oh honey," she says quietly.

"He's dumping me," I wail. "For some pliant, rat-faced little nurse *practitioner* who doesn't have an unusual bone in her body."

"What's her husband think about all this?" she asks.

"Who knows. He's probably *relieved*, wouldn't you say?"

We ponder this for a while. "I called him a couple of days ago and asked him if he missed me," I say.

"Uh-oh," Elizabeth says.

"He had one of his honesty attacks."

"Why, that little fuck," she starts. "I'd like to get my hands around his skinny *neck*."

"He's already left me," I say, "he's just too chicken to take his body with him."

"I know you don't want to hear this," she says carefully. "But it seems to me that you wouldn't be this upset about him wanting to leave you. I think you're this upset because *you* want to leave *him*." This makes my stomach lurch in a very sickening, grain-of-truth-to-it way.

"But I love him," I tell her. "He's the only man I've ever loved." Even I know how trite that sounds. I feel like a character in a Gothic novel.

"Keep in mind who you're talking to here," she says dryly.

"I can't believe I said 'He's the only man I've ever loved.' I'm supposed to be a *writer*, for God's sake." I might be starting to snap out of it.

"It's time for the other banana," she suggests. "And I'm gonna talk to you while you eat it."

Seventeenth summer, a farmhouse full of boys on the edge of town, a car full of girls heading toward it. It's Elizabeth's red convertible, prone to running out of gas and getting stuck in places that cars don't belong. As soon as we leave the city streets and hit the back roads, everyone except Elizabeth gets up and sits on the edge of the car instead of on the seats. When we go around curves there is a long moment where it feels like we might fall out and be run over by the back tires. We like this feeling. Because we're too young to die, we assume we won't. Also, alcohol is involved.

It's the year of Look Ma, No Bra, and extremely long blue jeans that drag on the ground and get caked with mud. Shoes are unheard of; hair is everything. We comb ours frantically as soon as the car stops. My own is long and lank, reaching just above my waist; it's useless to even try and restore order.

"Here." Renee takes my comb and starts working out the tangles gently, starting at the bottom. She raps me on the head with her knuckles when I tip my head back to finish my beer. "Stay still," she commands, in the voice she uses on the babies.

"Ouch," I say mildly.

Elizabeth assesses herself in the sideview mirror. She's trying to see if her rear end is sticking out. "Why do I have an egg-butt?" she asks. This is rhetorical.

Renee finishes my hair and asks if she should braid it. A vote is taken: two for the braid, two for leaving it down. I throw my vote in with leaving it, we do some last-minute adjustments, and then, making Janet go first because she has confidence, we step through the front door and into the farmhouse.

The living room walls are painted black and the furniture consists of a sprung couch with no cushions, an old dentist's chair, a black-light pole lamp, and a giant stereo system. Right now a guy named Dave is changing the album. Like a priest performing the sacrament, he kneels before the altar and removes the record from its sleeve. Holding the edges and blowing softly on it, he sets it on the turntable, moves the needle into place, and gently drops it. Deafening sound ensues.

Except for one guy named Bob, all the guys who live here are named either Steve or Dave, all have ponytails of varying lengths, and all worship Ted Nugent. They refer to him as Ted and speculate on his whereabouts constantly. They're a year or so older than us, high school graduates who are busy amounting to nothing. We all have crushes on one or another of them. Mine is in the kitchen right now, mixing up a concoction of lemonade and Everclear. He's a sweet-faced Steve with a charming personality and a massive drinking problem. He hardly ever notices me, but when he does I think I'm going to die. "Here," he says, handing me a plastic cup of potion. I take a sip and try not to shudder. It tastes like sugar-flavored eau de cologne. "Hey, that's good," I respond brightly. I'm working on having a better personality.

"Ted here yet?" he asks me.

"Uh, no," I reply. He wanders into the living room and I wait a second, then follow him.

Elizabeth and Janet are sitting on the funky couch reading album covers. Renee is on the floor, cross-legged, smoking a cigarette with her eyes closed. No sign of Carol. I look around. One of the Steves is missing as well. I drink some more of my medicine.

The music is so loud that the sound is distorted. I want to turn it down slightly, but I don't dare. It is an unspoken rule that girls don't touch stereo equipment. When the record ends there is a sudden leaden silence that rings almost as loudly as the music. Everyone looks startled and uncomfortable. A Dave gets up and pads over in his sock feet to put something else on. A different Dave loads a bong and passes it to his right. Someone switches off the regular light and switches on the black light. This is a relief for those of us who are worried about how we look; now everyone is equal, with velvety faces, lavender teeth and eyes.

The weed is laced with PCP; after two hits I feel like I'm in a hammock on the top deck of a gently rolling ocean liner. I stretch out on my back, using a stack of magazines for a pillow, and crawl inside the music. My head is an empty room, painted white, with high vaulted ceilings. There is a long beat of silence and then the sound of alarm clocks going off. I sit in a straight-backed chair in the middle of my head. Suddenly there is the pinging of a cash register and the sound of coins falling. I open my eyes briefly and see the rapt faces of the other revelers, the purple-toothed smile of a nodding Dave. I retreat back to the dark side of the moon. Money changes hands, guitars echo off the white walls.

When I come to it's some time later, there are more people around, blue-jeaned legs step over me from time to time. I like the party from this angle. Eventually my favorite Steve comes in and sits on the floor next to my head. He has another cup of poison for me. "You missed Ted," he hollers into my ear. In honor of trying to have a better personality, I make a disappointed face.

Although there are girls present, none of them seem to be my friends. "Where's Elizabeth?" I mouth to him. He leans in and puts his lips, then his tongue, to my ear. I pull my head away. "She's occupied," he yells, and gestures toward a closed door. When I ask where everybody else is he shrugs. I truly hate it when this happens.

As it turns out, Renee is in the kitchen, very stoned, doing the dishes. Three guys are sitting at the kitchen table, one cleaning pot, the other two watching Renee like she's a TV show. When she runs out of dishes, one of them obediently picks up another stack off the floor and sets them in the water for her. This place is a pig sty. I pour myself another cup of whatever that crap is.

Renee looks at me foggily, trying to assess my mood. "Want to dry some dishes?" she asks.

"Not hardly, pal," I say. The guys at the table give me a long look and I give them one back. A Dave holds out his hand to me.

"C'mere," he says kindly, pulling me onto his lap. The Beatles are on the stereo. "The Long and Winding Road," a song that'll break your heart in about one minute, begins to play. I sit quietly on the Dave's lap and hum a few bars. He pets my hair awkwardly for a while and then puts his hand up the back of my shirt. The other two guys exchange a smirk.

I take Dave's ear by the lobe and whisper into it. His eyes open wide. He puts his hand across his chest protectively as I get up. "She's *fierce*," he says to the other two. Renee drops some crusty silverware into the brown dishwater. She struggles for a second to bring me into focus.

"Jo Ann doesn't like that kind of stuff," she explains to them.

"Well, man oh man," Dave says. "What did *I* do." The other two laugh.

Looks like my old personality is back.

In the phone booth in New York, I draw a picture of a girl with her fists on her hips, eyebrows converging, mouth set. She's wearing my clothes. I have one question to ask Elizabeth, but first she wants to tell me about her weekend.

"I went out with a guy who looks like the Artful Dodger," she says. "He's in a band *and* he wears a top hat. He couldn't wear it on the date, though, because we went to a movie."

"That's good," I say. I tell her I'm working on a party scene.

"Which party?" she asks suspiciously. "What am I doing at it?"

"It's sort of a composite of all parties, you know?" There's silence at the other end. "It's just a *party* party, is all, with those guys who all had the same names."

"The Ted Nugent guys?" she asks.

Well, yes.

"I never liked any of those guys, did I?" she says hopefully.

Uh, I think Dave Nelson would be hurt.

She probes her brain, comes up with a memory. "Oh." She thinks for a second. "Well, he was a nice guy," she says firmly. "Wasn't he?"

We ponder for a minute and finally both admit we can't remember. I say they all look alike to me, and then instantly regret it, because I'm going to hear a lecture. Here it comes.

"Your attitude towards men s-u-x," she begins. "Look at me. I got divorced, too, and I'm not bitter."

Well, I'm willing to be bitter on both our behalfs. In the meantime, the one question I have to ask is Why were you always with guys and I never was?

"Because you were mean, that's why," she says gently. "Remember how mean you used to get?" This makes me feel awful. I was a mean person.

"You weren't a mean *person*," she says. "We were just weird back then. We were insecure."

But you weren't mean.

"Well, I had the exact opposite problem," she replies.

I light a cigarette illegally in the phone booth and try to blow the smoke into my coat pocket. The conversation goes on and on, more about the Artful Dodger. Meanwhile, back at the party, Renee shows me her pruny fingers.

"Exhibit A," she says. "This is exactly why you shouldn't take speed and go to a party." I pour her a cup of liquid nitrogen and she downs it quickly, the way she's doing everything else. "I keep thinking I want to clean the bathroom," she says.

"I'd steer clear if I were you," I advise her. "Five guys live here." She can see the wisdom in that.

Pretty soon Carol comes into the kitchen, blinking her eyes against the light. Her hair is a mess, her shirt is buttoned wrong, and she's been crying. He has hurt her feelings, which isn't hard to do. He forgot her name or something. "Let's go," she whispers. We rustle up Elizabeth and the three of us fade through the living room and out the door. The Steve I have a crush on is sitting on the front porch steps, smoking a joint, waiting for Ted. He reaches out and places his hand gently around my ankle. I stand there patiently until he lets go, and then continue down the steps. "See you," he says.

At the car, there is a moment of silence. Elizabeth tries to hand the keys off to me but I'm not in the mood. I climb in the back and hold on to my hair as we pull from the drive to the road. Carol stops crying and claims she's never going to another party. Elizabeth and I exchange a look in the rearview mirror. "In my whole entire *life*," she says emphatically, "so don't even try asking me to." The sky is full of diamonds, the moon is a narrow sliver, the road winds and curves, the drugs are wearing off. We left Renee and Janet at the party without a ride.

The voice of Motown comes on the radio and we sing quietly to ourselves. All the houses have their eyes closed as we sweep silently past them. Carol fixes her shirt, lights one cigarette off another, and I wave good-bye to them from the alley behind my house. Through the bushes, up the back walk, still humming. In the kitchen, two cookies and a long drink of water, up the stairs and into the bedroom. Across the hall my parents sleep peacefully behind their closed door, innocent as children.

On the way back from Florida I drive a hundred miles out of my way in order to visit my mother's grave. Small Illinois town where she grew up; the gas station, body shop, and ice cream parlor are owned by my uncles, on the edge of town a small barren cemetery is full of my dead relatives. My mother's tombstone is dark granite, on either side of it are pink geraniums, planted by my father. In front, beneath her name, is a coffee can full of wildflowers withering in the sun. Someone has been here before me, an aunt probably, driving past on her way into town from one of the nearby farms. The withering flowers prompt a maudlin scene in which I am both the actor and the audience. A red-tailed hawk circles overhead, a tractor chugs by on the highway, holding up a line of cars. A daughter weeps in the afternoon sunlight, a mother remains silent beneath a load of dirt.

Hours later my street appears in front of me, a tall catalpa tree, a child's scooter, and then the driveway where the husband stands, just off his bike, home from work. "Hi," he says cordially, putting an arm across my shoulders. And then, "I have a meeting tonight." His hand looks as white as paste next to my Florida arm. Inside, he goes into the study and closes the door. I hear the long beep of the answering machine as he listens to the messages and then erases them.

In bed that night I remain stationary as he toils in the darkness. Afterward, there is silence and the sound of breathing. Next to the bed, my big collie whines in her sleep. Finally, he says quietly, with something in his voice I don't recognize, "It's good you're back."

Tick, tock. Breathe in, breathe out. There is no mercy at this hour of the night, and my own voice sounds strange in the darkness. *I'm not*, is what I tell him. He rolls over and puts his face in the pillow. Everywhere you turn these days there's someone crying.

Billboards, fence posts, and cows go by at seventy miles an hour, a van honks as we pass it and someone gives us the finger in a friendly manner. We're caravaning our way to the rock quarries for a swimming party. Three cars and two vans are full of people and beer; I'm riding on back of a motorcycle, driven by my unofficial date, a charming madman named Wally. Wally is already in the party mood and so am I, because it's my nineteenth birthday. I have on a microscopic swimming suit, a Rolling Stones T-shirt, and Wally's helmet. He has on cut-off blue jeans, sunglasses, and a baseball cap. Every once in a while he'll holler, "Hold on!" and then execute an amazing maneuver that involves other vehicles on the road. I'm absolutely terrified, and keep imagining what skin on pavement would feel like. Nevertheless, I can't quit egging him on.

The water is like cold silk when you first get in. Elizabeth and I float ourselves around on air mattresses until we see a water snake swimming directly toward us with its head stuck up like a periscope. We take off for the beach and sun ourselves on an outcropping of rock. Somewhere in the vicinity, Wally is tapping the keg while others are running speaker wire. Eventually music comes forth and beer makes its way over to where we are. Guys start catapulting themselves into the water.

I get special treatment because it's my birthday. People keep calling me over to their cars and vans. "Here," they say generously. "Do some of this." In an effort to stay awake for my birthday, I decline almost everything. I'm a famous lightweight; even beer in the afternoon makes me sleepy. I stretch out on my rock and let the sun bake me while the others swim and get wasted. Elizabeth keeps up a running monologue next to me which I can tune in and tune out at will. Wally comes over to shake water on us from time to time; we bat him away like an insect.

Sometime during the early evening he produces three pills, one for each of us. "What are these?" I ask him. He looks at one of the pills closely, turning it over in his hand.

"'Lilly,'" he reads. "They're lilies, that's what. Red ones." Down the hatch.

Within an hour I'm singing a medley of Beatles tunes to anyone who will listen. My legs are not working correctly. "Hey, Jude," I say to the guy sitting next to me. His name is Tom. "Did you have any of those red lilies?" He doesn't know what I'm talking about. Elizabeth is nowhere in sight but I can see Wally off in the distance, slapping his leg and laughing silently and hysterically. He squints over in my direction and motions me to come hither. I point to my legs and shake my head. We give each other the peace sign.

There's a fire going, and some people are roasting things over it. I hear my name being called. "Liz is looking for you," Tom tells me. He stands, stretches, and heads for the beer. She comes tripping up, still in her swimming suit, with a man's workshirt over it. "Let's take a walk," she says. She's listing slightly to the right, but other than that, doing okay.

"I can't stand up," I tell her. I indicate the grass next to me. "You sit down."

We watch the other campers for a while, roasting their things, drinking their stuff, laughing and punching each other. "I can't stay here if you're going to sing," Elizabeth tells me. I stop singing.

Off in the distance the lizardy sound of Mick Jagger starts up, more cars arrive, people shout for no reason. The red lily has made me feel both weightless and heavy at the same time. The night air is cool against my sunburned arms. I can't remember what I did with my shoes. The only thing that would make me happier at this moment is if I could sing *Bang, bang, Maxwell's silver hammer*, but Liz won't let me. I try humming it softly but she starts to stand up so I have to cut it out. I wonder where Waldo is.

Renee and her boyfriend Pete emerge out of the darkness. She has my T-shirt and shoes. Even though my arms are balloon strings, I manage to get the shirt on and slip my swimming suit top off; the shoes I cannot even begin to contend with. Pete is short and very cool, with bedroom eyes, dark curly hair, and an uncivilized manner. Renee is working on taming him. He likes it that I took my swimming suit top off even though he didn't get a glimpse of anything. "Nice tits," he says generously. We send him to get beers but right before he leaves he bestows a big, fat birthday kiss on me. I dry my face on my T-shirt.

Here comes Janet, so tan her blond hair looks fake. She's got a concerned look on her face. Well, there's bad news. Wally's fiancée, Leeann, has just arrived unexpectedly. It was a surprise; she blew in from the north like bad weather, and now my birthday is wrecked. Everyone groans, including Tom and Pete, who like it when I'm in a good mood. *Bang bang Maxwell's silver hammer came down upon her head.* I shrug and put a decent face on it. I can't think of anything to sing.

At some point during the evening Wally catches my eye. Leeann is standing with her back to me, looking wifely and cruel. He holds his hands palms-up in the age-old gesture of *Hey, this is not my fault.* I look away with no expression on my face. Tom brings me a roasted marshmallow that burns the roof of my mouth. I lean my head on his knee and he pats my sunburned shoulder. It's my nineteenth birthday and here I am, Eleanor Rigby.

"She married him right out from under me," I say. We're back to the phone booth. All I have to do is close my eyes and I can see his long, pipe-cleaner legs, his hazel madman's eyes. He still remains the legendary good kisser.

She wants to know what made it legendary. I don't know; it was almost twenty years ago. Probably the fiancée in the background. "He was nuts," she says. Yeah, that didn't hurt either.

All the sweet, absent boys. Smoking jays like they were cigarettes. Playing their air guitars. Doling out their legendary kisses. We have a moment of long-distance silence for ourselves, perpetually the back-up singers.

"Hey, man," Elizabeth says, "speak for yourself."

It's 1976 or thereabouts. Feminism strikes suddenly, leaving destruction in its path. I've always had a tendency to be mean to men; now there's a reason for it. I'm learning to keep my hands in my pockets, so they won't see my fists.

Someone's living room, floor pillows, chamomile tea, soft-voiced women in painter's pants and big hoop earrings. Consciousness-raising. We learned why Susan B. Anthony should get her face on a coin. We learned that the speculum can be our friend. Some of us learned that the word *orgasm* actually described a real phenomenon.

"Hey," we said in unison.

I'm here to tell you that sisterhood is a powerful thing. We worked on constructing egos for ourselves; we tried to convince each other that our lives were worth inhabiting. We stopped shaving our armpits and gave ourselves wash-and-wear hairdos called shags. Occasionally, one of us would lob a beer can at the head of a deserving male. Feminism. The only down side I can remember is that the shags were hard to grow out.

The separate-but-equal principle held sway for a brief time. The guys who used to remove our clothes with their sliding glances dressed us right back up again when they saw our armpits. Women stalked out of the room when men accidentally called them honey. Eventually, though, we all calmed down a little and attempted to harmonize. Some lean-torsoed men tried to even the odds by putting on glittery eyeshadow and climbing up on platform heels to play their guitars. With the advent of cocaine, parties suddenly got livelier and longer.

Across the room, a guy navigates his way through the smoky throng to play with the equalizer. From there he goes to the front porch, where he adjusts a slide projector. This is his party, apparently. He's projecting slides of a David Bowie/Iggy Pop concert on the house across the street. There's a rivet punched through his ear lobe, a silver star, a small tribute to androgyny. He's simultaneously mellow and wired but he speaks thoughtfully and listens carefully. At some point, while one of us is talking, he presses his hand against the small of my back and doesn't move it. It stays there for more than a decade.

Some highlights. Early days: long evenings in the country house, I make drawings and smoke cigarettes, drink cups of tea. He stokes up the blue glass bong, plugs in an electric guitar, and plays "Secret Agent Man" over and over. We populate our house with dogs and have long, monotonous discussions about how to make them behave better. We go in the bedroom sometimes and close the door to get away from them, then feel sorry and open it again and let them boil up onto the bed and stick their noses in our faces. We do a wavery but heartfelt rendition of "Good Night, Irene" as we're driving, late, back from friends' houses. On a beach in South Carolina we lie on our backs and stare at the night sky and congratulate ourselves on getting along so well. Months later we discover grains of sand in the cuffs of his trousers, remember, and give each other secret, sappy looks.

We're pretty nice people for the most part, although neither of us ever sands off the edges we started out with. I am prone to my usual fits of melancholy and self-doubt; he has a tendency toward a manic energy that is enervating for anyone who beholds it. I have long ago lost all interest in drugs and alcohol but each evening he disappears inside a plume of smoke and emerges mellowed and distant. Rock and roll, of course, never dies. Sometimes very late at night we sit in the dark living room listening to the voices of various dead guys — Tommy Bolin, Jimi Hendrix, Bob Marley — while studiously ignoring each other. I observe that he isn't fully present past eight o'clock each night, and surprise myself by feeling grateful. I am left free to traipse around in my own psychic landscape. When we have fights he has a tendency to reply in baby-talk, which causes me to go berserk. I rant, then I rave, berating him in such florid terms that no one can keep a straight face. We get sheepish, we make up. The years tick by.

My lifelong addiction to books wanes, leaving me feeling

bored and bereft. Some time later I discover that I've left off reading them because I've decided to write them instead. He thinks this is a fine idea and supports it unconditionally, but finds that he is unable to read what I write because drowsiness overtakes him. I watch him several nights running as he nods and dozes, tries with an enormous effort to focus, and finally gives up. We agree without much discussion that it isn't necessary for him to read my writing. His own work is too consuming, he doesn't need one more task piled on top of the others. The match stops flaring, the bong stops bubbling, the old familiar chords of "Secret Agent Man" no longer bounce like tennis balls around the room. The dogs skulk into their corners.

His own work. Political organizing that begins on a power-to-the-people grassroots level and gradually works its way up to power-to-the-person. He educates the sheep and then becomes the shepherd. It's a rush to have them all listening, paying attention, laying down their votes. Another case where reefer has led to the hard stuff.

We're on the slippery slope now, it's only a matter of time. It's women galore. He begins to look at me with an appraising eye. Familiarity, that good friend of contempt, makes me seem plain as dishwater. Once when we fight over something and apologize later, he admits that he might have been a bit stern with me. For hours the word hangs in the air above my head like a grand piano. *Stern*. He might have been stern with me. I realize that one of the reasons he doesn't want children is that he thinks he already has one. I start listening to how he talks to others compared to how he talks to me. In a crowded room one night I catch myself getting ready to take him by the necktie and heave him up against the wall. I feel like a rabid dog, but I smile placidly and make idle chat with the wife of his best friend, the future chiseler. In the car on the way home I say to him in the most dangerous tone I can come up with, *"You have got to treat me like an equal."* The wiper blades clock back and forth, car lights bear down and then pass. He says, looking straight ahead through the glistening windshield, simply and sadly, "I can't."

An update on the Artful Dodger. Turns out he's our age and has a day job, besides playing the drums.

"Well, you've gotta love a guy in a band," I say encouragingly.

"I agree," she says. "I just wish he played the *guitar."*

A woman walks by the phone booth in a nightgown, carrying a coffee cup and a cigarette. It's early afternoon. I knock on the glass and wave hello. There are any number of eccentrics around here. She's a painter.

Here's a good one: After the divorce I was on my way somewhere early one morning and saw Eric's brand-new girlfriend walking from his house to her own, wearing nothing but a pale lavender nightgown and a pair of Birkenstock sandals. Her hair was stuffed into a rubber band and hung down her back like a horse's tail, she was holding a sheaf of papers and a long leash, at the end of which was her dog, a big black biter. The nightgown was one of those Indian-style jobs, with embroidery along the bodice. It's the sort of thing you could convince yourself didn't look *totally* like a nightgown if you only had three blocks to walk and it was too early for anyone to be out driving around. Except I was. Out driving around. I spent the rest of the morning draped over someone's couch, sobbing and eating cinnamon toast.

I tell Elizabeth about this. Yeah, yeah, she remembers. Well, never again, I vow. Thank God *that's* in my past. Who *needs* it. Blah blah blah. The boys of my youth give me the malaise.

"Oh brother," she says.

Don't oh brother me. And I gotta go, I'm late for my nap.

The truth is, I'm weary of all that men stuff. It's either so boring that I'd rather hang around with my girlfriends or it's like gunfire to the chest. I actually *like* it inside the bell jar — I don't have to breathe anyone's air but my own and I still get a view of the landscape. There's a woman here at the colony, Stasia, a filmmaker who went to a workshop to learn how to walk over a bed of hot coals. She tells me about it postnap, as we're waiting for the dinner bell, having drinks on the terrace. The thing is, why would anyone want to walk over a bed of hot coals?

"I saw a flyer for it on a lamppost," she explains.

They spent an afternoon in the presence of a short charismatic man, talking about their feelings and consulting various higher powers. At about four-thirty they took their shoes off and performed the miracle. So, what did it feel like?

"It felt like hot coals," she says.

I knew it would.

The door to the terrace swings open and out walks our friend Frank. Right behind him is a new guy. Frank immediately starts filling us in on how much work he got done during the day. I feel vaguely guilty about the magnitude of my afternoon nap. Somehow the quality of the light has changed on the terrace, there's a dangerous peach glow coming over the horizon. The new guy is introducing himself to a group of people. There are handshakes around. Today Frank finished a painting and started two new ones. Stasia says that you don't burn your feet because the coals are too light. The new guy looks over in this direction. It's like when you put your hand in a hot oven; the coals are almost light as air, they're hot but have very little density so they don't burn you. I can feel the frayed edge of his denim jacket and he's standing all the way over there. I look at my hand. Frank asks me how the boys of my youth are doing.

"They're boring," I say absently. Here he comes.

———

Pertinent details. Blond poet. A slightly jaded and weary air about him. Something recognizable in the sideways glance, the set of the shoulders. He's sober now, but from what I can tell the former bad boy is buried in a shallow grave. The color of his eyes escapes me but not the quality of the gaze. He appears to be fully and alarmingly present at all times. I have to get out of here.

He leaves me a note on the mail table, full of charming misspellings. We meet and walk, describe our lives. He puts his hand on my arm as we cross a street and continues listening, offering kindness and advice. I have a sudden overwhelming desire to touch his face. I put my hands in the pockets of my jeans. It feels crowded inside my bell jar; condensation forms and I begin weeping. He watches calmly, one foot on the bumper of a car. At some point he reaches out, lightly touches my face.

I take to wearing a Walkman and earphones everywhere I go, piping music directly into my head. The phone booth is the only place it doesn't work.

"I can only talk for a minute," I tell her. My days are numbered here; I feel a longing for my empty living room, for the grizzled face of Sheba the dog. The blue enamel breakfast table, the rug with a picture of New Zealand on it, the bird's nest we found outside the country place years ago, made from hair shed by my old dead heroic-hearted collie. I'm tired of being here. I miss my stuff.

"I'm sick of *my* stuff," she says. "I want all new everything."

I want I want I want. I want to go home.

"What's going on?" she asks. After a short pause a lightbulb goes on over her head. "Uh-oh," she says.

Yeah.

"Heck," she says cheerfully. "That's *good*. Is he nice?"

I don't think I know what nice means these days. "Well, he hasn't pulled a gun on me," I tell her. She sighs.

I've spent my whole life in this phone booth. I want my circus footstool, my pink coffee table, my Albert Payson Terhune books. I want my Bruce Springsteen records. The Walkman lies dormant in my lap. I push the On button and the tiny voice of Van Morrison emanates from the earphones. "The thing is," I tell her, "he already has a brown-eyed girl. Back home." Thank God.

"Oh." She's thinking this over. "Hmmmm."

A pall settles over the conversation. I stare at my reflection, distorted in the chrome of the telephone. "This is still my youth," I finally tell her.

"Uh, whatever you say." She sounds skeptical.

I peer closer at the chrome mirror. My vertical wrinkle is still visible and it's afternoon. It's usually faded back into my face by mid-morning. Also, I might be getting jowls.

"I'm looking at my vertical wrinkle in the telephone," I say.

"Isn't it supposed to be gone by now?" she asks. "It's one o'-clock."

"I hate to break it to you, but it's two o'clock here," I inform her. "I need oil-of-old-ladies." I can't even bring myself to mention the jowls, for which there's no cure anyway. All the women in my family begin to look like bulldogs right around the age of thirty-eight; it's a legacy.

The Artful Dodger has taken a turn for the worse. "He's religious," Elizabeth says. "And not only that, but he thinks I'm going to church with him this Sunday." Oh boy. To my way of thinking, the problem isn't necessarily that he's religious; it's more that he doesn't have anything to counter it with, like a drinking problem or weird sexual tastes. "Well, actually he is a little weird in that category," she admits. This livens up the conversation for a few minutes.

Before leaving the phone booth I plug the music back into my head. More hollering from Van. I notice as I set out on my walk that the New York landscape has taken on the blurred and sepia tones of a distant memory. I'm already back in Iowa, waiting for my body to join me.

Once home, I discover that I'm bored. Outside, long blank fields of corn and the blue midwestern sky. Inside, the same dustballs in the same corners. The cat carries tiny corpses up to the back step and arranges them in rows. The kid next door plays basketball with earphones on in his driveway, mouthing lyrics that would turn your hair white if you could hear them. Squint your eyes and he looks a little bit like Dave Anderson. Close your eyes altogether and the blond poet appears.

I perfect the art of brooding, gazing for hours at the paint on my living room ceiling, smoking and smoking. Elizabeth comes to visit me one weekend and we try on each other's clothes and paint our toenails maroon.

"I'll say one thing," she remarks. "I do happen to have decent *feet*." And she turns them this way and that, admiring.

My own feet look like they belong to a stranger with too much time on her hands. I stretch out on the couch and feed myself a potato chip. There is a long hair-sized crack running down the center of the ceiling.

"Don't brood in *front* of me," she says.

Mister Spider has built a web right above my giant, dying, phallic-looking cactus. It's a little trampoline and he's bouncing around in the center of it right now. Even the spiders are bored.

"It could be worse," she mentions. "We could be having to

entertain those two mopes." She means our ex-husbands, the Jim and Eric show.

If they were here, this is what they'd be doing: nothing, that's what. They'd be placidly sitting around, waiting for us to make something happen.

"So we'd still be bored," she concludes, "*and* we wouldn't even be able to paint our toenails, for fear of ridicule." It's true. Not only would it be boring but I'd have that old feeling back of constantly imagining myself as a widow wearing a great outfit. The phone rings.

"Who could be calling me here?" Elizabeth says.

We let it ring and ring until the answering machine kicks in and then we tiptoe over to listen. "This is what I do when you call," I tell her.

My answering machine voice lies about my whereabouts and then the beep comes on. Suddenly I'm standing on my circus footstool like a mouse has been let loose in the room. It's the guy.

"Hi, Jo Ann, this is X," he says and then leaves a long, rambling, totally coherent message and hangs up. Oh man. He's shimmering in my living room like a genie released from a bottle.

I don't know whether to faint or kill myself. Elizabeth laughs unbecomingly. I put both hands around my own neck. We do our silent screaming routine.

We are no longer bored.

ABOUT THE AUTHOR

Jo Ann Beard's work has appeared in *The New Yorker, Tin House,* and *Best American Essays*. She has received a Whiting Award and fellowships from the Guggenheim Foundation and the New York Foundation for the Arts.

. . . AND HER MOST RECENT NOVEL

In April 2011 Little, Brown and Company will publish Jo Ann Beard's *In Zanesville*. Following is an excerpt from the novel's opening pages.

We can't believe the house is on fire. It's so embarrassing first of all, and so dangerous second of all. Also, we're supposed to be in charge here, so there's a sense of somebody not doing their job.

"I told you to go up there and see what they were doing," Felicia says.

"I told *you* to go up there," I reply.

We've divided the kids up, three each, and two of hers were upstairs playing with matches while the third, and all of mine, were secured in the backyard.

The smoke isn't too bad at this point; basically it smells like a campfire. We still can't find where it's coming from, although the third-floor bathroom is a pretty safe bet, if we listen to Renee, who is accusing Derek of setting a toilet paper fire in a wicker wastebasket.

There is no sign of Derek anywhere; he set the fire and moved on to the next thing. Renee, loitering in the hallway, had played Barbie until the last possible moment and then gave up when the smoke began swirling, calling out, "Fire!" in an annoyed voice.

"He said if I told, he'd murder me," she trilled, loping down the stairs and out, eluding us.

We've been babysitting for the Kozaks all summer, five days a week, eight hours a day; six kids—Derek, Renee, Stewart, Wanda, Dale, Miles—and various other, easier-to-control creatures: a tarantula, a python, a rat snake, some white mice, and an elderly German shepherd with bad hips who lies in the dirt next to the doghouse all day, licking his stomach. We each get seventy-five cents per hour, which doesn't sound like enough when we're here but blooms into an incredible bounty on the weekends, when we're lying around trying to decide how to spend it. Almost a dollar an hour, accumulating slowly and inexorably, in a revolving series of gagging diaper changes, nose wipings, placing of buzzing flies in the tarantula's terrarium, assembly-line construction of baloney-cheese-mayonnaise sandwiches, folding of warm laundry, chipping of egg crust off the vinyl tablecloth, benevolent dispensing of Sno-Kone dimes, helpless shouting, appalling threats, and perusal of their porn library.

We are fourteen, only three years older than Derek, who is the oldest of the Kozak children. Derek isn't much work because he disappears for most of each day, showing up only when the parents are due back home, which is fine with us. He won't mind, he cusses, and he once threw a handful of worms at us after a rainstorm. The other five kids range in age from one and a half to nine; some in fact claim to be the same age, although none of them look even vaguely alike. We can't figure it out, but then again, we don't try to.

*   *   *

"Man, are we in for it," Felicia says, panting.

We're evacuating the pets. She's struggling with the smaller snake aquarium, which houses, along with the python, the python's furniture—a bent log, a plastic bowl, and a rock for the mice to hide behind. The snake, a young albino, is gently probing its ivory nose at the jumbo box of ice cream sandwiches we've put on top to hold the wire mesh lid in place.

I've got the tarantula cage under one arm and all seven white mice, which are riding in a pillowcase. Once outside, I go through the gate, past the semicollapsed garage into the alley to where the sticker bushes are, set the pillowcase down, and give it a poke. The mice nose their way out and disappear into the bramble.

"The mice just escaped," I announce to the kids as I come back through the gate.

"Wanda ate gum off the fence," Dale reports.

Wanda is hanging upside down from the rusty jungle gym. She opens her mouth and something purple lands in the dirt. "Dale stole money," she calls out.

"Shut up and stay there," I tell them.

"Our mom said if you told us to shut up one more time, she'd shut *you* up for good," Renee informs me. This has the unmistakable ring of truth to it—her mother has a thatch of black hair that she sets on hot curlers every morning, and once when she was taking out the curlers, she said, "Look," and when I looked she had popped out her false tooth and was leering like a jack-o'-lantern.

So far, no smoke is visible outdoors, but when we go back inside, the hallway is swirling, and it stinks quite a bit, more like a toilet paper fire now than a campfire. It takes both of us to handle the rat snake aquarium; we're staggering, trying not to breathe, but we both hate the rat snake and are scared it will get loose, so we stop and rescue some food to pile on top—a box of cereal and some flat packages of cheese—and then lug it toward the door.

The snake, agitated, puts his head under a corner of the lid, and about four inches of him leaks out, right near my hand. I start screaming and then Felicia sees him undulating there and starts screaming too. For a moment, we revolve in panicked circles, holding the aquarium between us and screaming. The sound is so loud and frightening in the narrow, smogged hallway that we calm down and use a package of cheese to direct him back inside where he belongs.

"Now what are we supposed to do?" Felicia asks, once we're outside.

The children, clustered by their swing set, stare over our heads. Behind us, like a dragon, their house has begun to exhale long tendrils of smoke.

Forget fathers, forget teachers: our mothers are the ones with the answers, the only people who know something about everything, although it's true that the answers are never that great and that both mothers are incredibly bossy and both have at least one disturbing trait. For Felicia's mother, it's a bad back that can go out on a moment's notice, freezing her in place; for my mother, it's a deep manlike voice that frightens people. Felicia's mother, Phyllis, works downtown at an optometrist's office, answering the phone and polishing eyeglasses; my mother works near the river at a cement company, typing and doing accounting.

We call Phyllis about any issue involving the kids and their behavior, and call my mom about anything having to do with food or household troubles. Both mothers are in the dark—obviously—about the snakes, the furred spider, the pink-nosed mice, and the occasional late-afternoon visits by a rival motorcycle gang called the Cherry Pickers.

We call the Kozak parents about nothing; we don't even know where they go during the day, each of them riding off on their own motorcycle. Yvonne wears green hospital scrubs and black leather chaps; Chuck wears jeans that fasten somewhere underneath his stomach, and tall clanking boots with buckles; they both wear leather jackets year-round that say *King Dong* on the back.

"Sand and Gravel," my mom says in her at-work voice. "How may I help you?"

"Hi," I say. I'm in the back hallway with my head out the door, the phone cord stretched as far as it will go.

"Uh-oh," she says over the sound of typewriters, her own and that of her co-workers, Trish and Char, women my mother mentions incessantly around the house. "Now what?"

Once I tell her, there's no way around something hideous happening. I knew we should've called Phyllis, who is more erratic but also pliant. A toxic cloud of smoke is starting to come out the doorway, swirling past us into the bright summer air of the cluttered yard. Felicia raises her eyebrows at me and steps backward, down the porch steps.

"What, quick, I'm busy," my mom says, lighting a cigarette into the telephone.

"Well," I say. "Something's on fire here."

"What do you mean, something's on fire?" she barks. All the background typing stops.

"There's *some* smoke, not too much," I say.

"Don't say *some*," Felicia hisses. "Say *lots*, but that it was Derek, not us."

"I heard that," my mother says quickly. "Where are the kids?"

"Out," I say.

"Where are you?" she asks.

"In," I say.

"Get out *right now*," she tells me.

"Don't call the fire department," I plead.

"Out," she says. "And get those kids far away from the house."

"This is embarrassing!" I cry, slamming the phone down.

We move the children to the next-door neighbor's yard, a place so beautifully mowed and toyless that it might as well be in another dimension. The man, Mr. Vandevoort, uses a table knife to make a narrow moat between the grass and the sidewalk; Mrs. Vandevoort grows rosebushes along the side of the house and petunias in a painted tire. She wears white ankle socks and comes out briskly clapping her hands whenever a crow settles on the lawn. It's a good thing they're at work, because they would not like knowing that the Kozak children are standing on their grass. We set the snakes and the spider under their picnic table and frantically call Lurch, the German shepherd, over and over, until he gets to his feet, hobbles across the yard, and stares through the open gate.

"You're gonna get burned up!" the children shriek at him. Stewart sprints over, tugs on the dog's collar twice, and then gives up and sprints back. Lurch sits down and cocks his head, listening, then points his nose into the air and makes a high, thin howl.

A siren can be heard off in the distance.

As it turns out, the firemen, who we were afraid of, are nicer than my own mother, who we both are and aren't afraid of. She pulls up in the Oldsmobile, smoking a cigarette and accompanied by Trish and Char, also smoking cigarettes. At that point the firemen have already unrolled their hose and carried it inside the house. They haven't even bothered to latch their boots, and in fact behave more like garbage men, swinging on and off their truck, banging things around, and carrying on conversations that aren't about fire.

Right as my mother and her friends pile out of the car, the firemen begin breaking all the windows in the third floor. My mother stares upward, through dark green sunglasses.

"Goddamn it," she says.

Felicia and I have now joined the ranks of the children; we stand side by side on the Vandevoorts' grass, me holding Miles in his wet diaper, Felicia with her hands over Wanda's ears. Shattering glass and shouted orders for two minutes and then it's over.

"Hi, I'm responsible for these two," my mother explains to the fireman in charge, pointing at us. "They're only fourteen."

You can tell he's the chief because he looks like a fireman from a television show. He has carried forth from the house the charred skeleton of a wicker wastebasket and a molten hunk of turquoise plastic that used to be the diaper pail.

"The fire was contained to the third-floor bathroom," he tells her. "And it wasn't even a fire, actually, although we soaked the room pretty extensively—you just have to," he explains apologetically. "It looks like what they said: matches and toilet paper. This thing"—he inclines his head toward the melted plastic pail, a hunk of brown diaper still visible—"is where the noxious smell came from. Second and first floors, they need some fans going for a couple of hours and it'll clear out okay. We gave them free air-conditioning on the third floor."

My mother and her friends talk in low voices while the men roll up the hose and kick the shards of glass off the driveway. One of the ones wearing his rubber coat open over an undershirt points to the bare feet of the children and then to the glass. Feet, glass. Get it? The children nod obediently, struck dumb by the dazzling celebrity of all this.

Miles, clasped against my dampening T-shirt, takes a plastic shovel out of his mouth and points it at the big red truck in the driveway.

"Fire fuck," he whispers.

My mother takes her colleagues back to the office and then returns with two old, clattering fans to add to the ones that are already going, and a grocery sack full of worn-out bath towels. When all the fans are set up it's like a terrible, rattling wind tunnel, smelly, and then my mother makes me and Felicia wipe down the front hall with damp rags.

The kids sit at the kitchen table while my mother scrubs the vinyl tablecloth and then makes them lunch from what she finds in the icebox.

"We're having chicken!" Stewart cries.

"It's tuna fish, poophead," Wanda says. She looks at my

mother with a mixture of challenge and awe. "Huh? He's got poop on his head."

"*Hey,*" my mother says. She stares down at Wanda until Wanda closes her eyes, picks up her sandwich, and takes a bite, then sets it back down, half on the plate and half on the tablecloth.

"She's blind," says Dale helpfully. "She can't even see the poop on her *own* head."

"If I hear any more of that, you'll all be spanked," my mother says. "I don't fool around."

"They're finally gonna get it," I whisper to Felicia. Our bucket is full of black, oily water now and we're done cleaning, just waiting for my mother to leave, slapping at the walls and the baseboards only when she walks by the doorway.

"*We're* the ones who are gonna get it," Felicia whispers back. "We burned up their house."

For a moment, we both have an image of Chuck, in his boots and cracked leather jacket, the overhang of the stomach, the walrus mustache, the way we have seen him grab Yvonne by the waist in order to say something in her ear. She's not exactly petite, either—Felicia saw her pick up Stewart by the neck once and give him a toss. In going through their dresser drawers, we've come across black-and-white photos of Yvonne and Chuck and some of their friends, all stark naked in a variety of shocking tableaus. The pictures are mostly of couples and groups, squirming around on gray bedclothes or outside on blankets with rocks in the background—all except one, of an older woman wearing a sailor's hat and nothing else. She's lying on a bed grinning into the camera and saluting. We used to stare at it every few days for a long time, trying to make sense of her pose, her expression, the deep dirtiness of the whole endeavor. Then one day she showed up at the house, with a very large teenage girl in blue jeans. The two of them sat on the back steps, smoking and drinking Pepsi, and ended up leaving right before Yvonne and Chuck came home. The older woman was wearing a tank top and she didn't have on a sailor hat, but it was definitely her.

We can't even anticipate what these people are capable of. Derek is missing, my mother is trespassing, the house is coated in soot, the ice cream bars are melted. Felicia begins to cry.

"Don't cry or she'll never leave," I beg in a whisper.

"W-w-w-we're deh-heh-head," she sobs. "*Deh*-heh-head."

A crowd appears in the doorway, the kids clustered behind my mother.

"No use in crying, Flea," she says briskly. "This isn't your doing, it's theirs." She means Derek, Yvonne, Chuck, the entire crew of Kozaks, for calling all this attention to themselves. The children gaze up at her, a tall, sandwich-making woman with a deep voice who can make the babysitters mind.

"She better go home," Renee suggests to my mother. "Right?"

"Wrong," my mother replies.

Go home! Home, where it's somebody's job to babysit *us*. We wish fervently that we'd listened to ourselves and not taken this job. All to get clothes! Specifically, a pair of tweed wool culottes with a matching jacket for me and a navy blue sweaterdress for Felicia. Those are the outfits that started the whole problem, which has now expanded to fisherman's sweaters, Nehru shirts, two-toned Capezios, a plaid wool miniskirt, green corduroy flannel-cuffed shorts, et cetera. And all on layaway at the Style, a store we wouldn't even have the nerve to go into if we weren't hopped up on all this income.

We do enjoy our Saturdays, though, after a hard workweek. Our pattern is to sleep late, at one or the other of our houses, and then walk uptown to eat at Weigandt's, a soda fountain run by a family with prominent noses. Even their littlest kids have to work there, counting jelly beans and putting them in Baggies with twist ties; their grandmother sits slumped at the cash register with her hands tucked in her armpits; one of their teenagers waits on us. I always order the same thing: iced tea with sugar and two bananas sliced into a bowl of mayonnaise. Felicia gets navy bean soup, fried baloney, and the same thing as me to drink. From there, we walk downtown to shop at the Style, picking out new items and laying them away along with the old ones; then we go to Carlson's, our downtown's department store, to use the bathroom on the fifth floor, which has pale blue carpeting that I once threw up on. Then we go to the dime store and poke through bins of crap—buttons, hairnets, shoehorns, clothespins—until we're in a bad mood; then we go to Felicia's mom's office and wait to get a ride back up the hill with her.

The optometrist's office is grubby and stale, with withered, dusty plants climbing all over inside the front window, and the optometrist himself wears thick, smudged glasses; it's like peering into a pond to look him in the eye.

"Here they are again," he always says, leaning out from behind his curtain. "Frick and her friend Frack."

Felicia's mom's working at an optometrist's office is why Felicia had contact lenses before anyone else had even heard of them. They are virtually invisible and yet still have to be located when they pop out onto the floor or float off their mark, drifting like unmoored rafts into the farthest bloodshot reaches of her eyeballs.

My mother disapproves of the whole concept of contact lenses—the idea of putting a shard of glass in your eye! "I don't know what Phyllis is thinking," she said. "This doctor has her over a barrel."

"It's a new thing!" I tried to explain.

"Yes," she replied, arching a brow. "They've got to have the crème de la crème over there." She'd never forgiven Felicia's mother for buying a blue fur couch and armchair. Not fur like a real animal, but fur like a stuffed animal.

Right now the smoke and the crying have irritated Felicia's eyes to the point where she has to switch to glasses, turning her into an earlier horn-rimmed version of herself. She immediately resumes the unconscious habit of wrinkling her nose upward to reset the heavy glasses when they slip down.

"Here comes the witch of witcherton," she says, staring at herself in the hall mirror. Actually, if one of us is good looking, it's her. She's tall and elegant, green eyed, although her teeth are slightly out of order, and she isn't particularly neat.

I, on the other hand, am neat, but that's about it. The body is wrong, scrawny; the face is pale and nondescript under its suntan. I talk with a faint sibilance that people think comes from the gap between my front teeth but that actually comes from me trying to be like Dee Jurgenmeyer, a girl from my childhood who had a real lisp. Once I started it, I couldn't stop, even when they sent us both to speech therapy and Dee was cured. The hair is the best feature, limp but long and silky. I don't particularly like having nice hair, though, because it gives people the wrong impression about me.

It's like a mysterious stranger I saw in a movie once, who everyone thought was a beautiful lost child in a red cape. From a distance all you could see besides the swirling cape was a head of lustrous hair. A man finally grabbed the child by the hood and turned it around and it was a leering dwarf; the man screamed, and everyone at the movie screamed too. That's why I mostly wear my hair in braids.

In fact, my mother does finally return to work, after taking it upon herself to leave her phone number and a note of explanation on the kitchen table. She also put the kids down for naps, something we never even bothered trying before.

"That's a good way to get a fire started," Felicia says as they troop upstairs.

As soon as my mother's gone, we tear up her note and the phone number. One by one the children drift back downstairs to stare at us.

"That lady was mean," Wanda says admiringly.

Dale is staring out the window. Suddenly he bolts for the back door. "Here come the cops!" he shrieks. "Here come the cops!"

The children disperse like vapor, all but Miles, who clings to my leg, sobbing.

There's a cop on the front porch, fitted out with a gun and holster. Felicia and I open the door together; Miles goes limp and lets me lift him off my leg and onto my hip.

"Who's in charge here?" the cop asks.

"The parents are, but they aren't home," Felicia says in a whisper. "We're here right now, but her mother was in charge." She gestures toward me and quickly retreats behind her hair, the straw curtain.

"She stepped out," I lie. Felicia nods vigorously at the floor.

"So, you the babysitters?" he asks.

"We were, we aren't sure now," Felicia says evasively. She looks steadfastly past the barbered edges of his head. Behind him, next to the door, is a round leaded-glass window with a number of BBs lodged in it.

"You didn't call the fire department when you had a fire," the cop states, as though he's reading it off a police report. "Out of 'embarrassment,' that right?"

"No," I say. "We did call." He's slightly fat and has got several things swinging from his waistline, including a radio, a leather nightstick, a long-handled flashlight, and a pair of handcuffs.

"Well, next time keep in mind," he says, "you could end up literally dying of embarrassment."

"We called!" Felicia insists, looking at him directly for the first time. In fact, glaring. "How else do you think the firemen got here?"

He stares at us, chewing a thin strand of gum, one hand resting on the knob of his nightstick. We stare back for a while and then give up and look off to the side. "I need to talk to the boy who started the blaze," he says finally.

"We don't know where he is," I tell the cop. "Nobody knows."

A voice comes ringing down from above. "He's at Victor's!" Renee calls out. A moment later she appears on the landing, wearing a swimsuit and a pair of boots. "He thinks the whole house is burned down."

"Well, I'll be sure and let him know," the cop says generously, "if you tell me where Victor lives."

She stares down at us, scratching at her leg inside the rubber boot. The cop looks at me.

"Tell him, Renee," I order her.

She turns and runs up again, into the farthest reaches of the ruined house.

Felicia sighs and heads outside the back way; Miles puts his hands on my cheeks and turns my face toward his. "Cah?" he asks moistly.

"Cop," I tell him, and then feel confused. Is that wrong, to say cop? "Policeman," I clarify.

Felicia returns in half a minute with Stewart; she's got his arm twisted behind his back so he has to walk sideways up the front steps.

"Okay, I don't like to see that," the cop tells her. She lets him go.

Stewart's face is streaked with tears, and his white hair is pressed against his pale pink head. His shorts are a size too small. He tugs at the front of them.

"Let me ask you, pal," the cop says to Stewart. He moves closer and then tries to crouch, but his gear rides up on him. He puts a knee down to steady himself. "Can you tell me where Victor lives?"

Stewart nods.